'This is a book for everyone. It turns out that, like breathing or running, conversation is actually a skill that can be learned. *Watch Your Language* is an essential read to help you have better and more useful conversations.'
James Alexander MBE, Chair of Finance Earth

'One of the most asked questions in my work is, "How can I get better at having difficult conversations?" No one seems to have this skill nailed down and it is a daily challenge in our lives. Rob gives a masterclass in how to navigate this tricky maze. I would suggest you get your highlighter out, because this book is full of simple, practical and impactful tools.'
Dr Kate Goodger, performance psychologist for Team GB at six Olympic Games and Group Head of Innovation and Performance at Laing O'Rourke

'Rob is a rare find – not only is he smart in terms of IQ but he has an abundance of EQ. He can instinctively understand, interpret and coach people to vastly improve their communication skills and their relationships. *Watch Your Language* shows you how to do this in practical, bite-sized chunks – the next best thing to having Rob pull up a chair alongside you.'
Sarah Tanner, Group Head of People at Pixomondo

'*Watch Your Language* is essential reading for any organization seeking a collaborative culture.'
Nigel White, Executive Vice-President for Project Oversight, SNC-Lavalin

'Speaking to Rob has helped me become a better footballer and a better person. He encourages me to find the answers to my own questions and challenges. His guidance is still effective weeks, months and years later.'
Sam Field, professional footballer, Queens Park Rangers F.C.

'Language brings meaning into existence and this is where the problems start for us as human beings – our listening and interpretations cause us to get stuck. I have had the privilege of working with Rob for many years and his techniques will enable you, and your organisation, to have better conversations and to keep moving toward your desired outcomes and goals.'
Lisa White, Director of People and Culture, The Crown Estate

'I have learned that powerful conversations are essential to world-class performance. Receiving encouragement and having challenging conversations with my coach and team members have been absolutely vital to my success. This book will show you how.'

Amy Williams MBE, Olympic gold medallist

'Rob's new book *Watch Your Language* provides highly practical tools to advance our psychological evolution through being cooperative rather than competitive in our communication with each other.'

Sir John Whitmore, author of the bestselling *Coaching for Performance*

'*Watch Your Language* reveals how the way we think influences the way we communicate. This is cutting-edge psychology packaged in the most accessible way. Anyone who is serious about improving their communication skills will find it practical and relevant.'

Dr Rob Archer, The Career Psychologist

'Rob's book will teach you how to hear what's really being said and say what you really mean to say. It will help you to increase your self-confidence and to put your relationships on a firmer and more positive footing. As texts, emails and other forms of "silent" communication crowd out the opportunity to practise the art of face-to-face conversation, we need the help of a skilled communicator more than ever. I recommend Rob's book to anyone who wants to communicate more effectively.'

Dr Linda Blair, clinical psychologist, author, columnist, broadcaster

'Rob understands the dynamics of conversation inside out. He has vast experience and mastery in this field. The world will be better for him sharing it.'

Hugh Brasher, Race Director, London Marathon

'*Watch Your Language* offers a truly fascinating insight into the complex world of conversation.'

Martin Davies, bestselling author of *The Conjuror's Bird*

WATCH YOUR LANGUAGE

WATCH YOUR LANGUAGE

Why Conversations Go Wrong and How to Fix Them

ROB KENDALL

WATKINS

Sharing Wisdom
Since 1893

Watch Your Language

Rob Kendall

First published as *Blamestorming* in the UK and USA in 2014 by Watkins,
an imprint of Watkins Media Limited

This edition published in the UK and USA in 2023
by Watkins, an imprint of Watkins Media Limited
Unit 11, Shepperton House, 83–93 Shepperton Road
London N1 3DF

enquiries@watkinspublishing.co.uk

Design and typography copyright © Watkins Media Limited 2014, 2023
Text copyright © Rob Kendall 2014, 2023

10 9 8 7 6 5 4 3 2 1

Printed in the United Kingdom by TJ Books Ltd
Typeset by Andrew Chapman
Illustrated by Richard Horne
Illustration on page 174 by Sneha Alexander

A CIP record for this book is available from the British Library

ISBN: 978-1-78678-789-7 (Paperback)
ISBN: 978-1-78678-791-0 (eBook)

www.watkinspublishing.com

CONTENTS

CHAPTER
ONE

BE CURIOUS

Laying the Foundations for More Rewarding Conversations

Language is one of the great wonders of being human. Around 70,000 years ago, our ancestors made the leap into language and never looked back. Prior to that, they communicated through a lexicon of rudimentary vocalizations, but the full-blown flowering of language unlocked a multitude of benefits. In a spectacularly short space of time our forebears started to think and collaborate in ways that were previously inconceivable and gained a remarkable advantage over other species. You and I are the downstream recipients of their legacy, and so is the world we inhabit.

Fast-forwarding to the present day, we conduct our lives through conversation of one kind of another. Whether it happens face-to-face, on the phone, by email or via instant messaging, it's something we mostly take for granted. While we navigate through our social landscape with extraordinary dexterity, life serves up its fair share of misunderstanding and disagreement.

In fact, conversations get tangled up all the time. What you'd thought would be a straightforward chat with your partner turns into a flaming row. Your teenager reacts to a well-intended comment and storms out. A work meeting feels like a waste of time because no one is actively listening. You prepare what you want to say in a tricky dialogue but can't find your voice when you need it. In each case, you struggle afterwards to pin down precisely who said what, or where the conversation broke down, and the process repeats itself.

Thankfully, there's no need to resign ourselves to daily frustration. Every conversation offers us the chance to make small changes in language, context or tone which – when repeated over time – turns the tide on our relationships and our productivity. To identify which conversational dials to turn up, and which to turn down, we need to recognize where and how things go wrong.

TRICKY SITUATIONS

Watch Your Language focuses on four fundamental situations. Each of them is the unwanted outcome of a conversation that's gone wrong:

1. The Tangle – where crossed wires lead to uncertainty and confusion, uncoordinated action and frustrated expectations.

How often do you shake your head in bewilderment and wonder how on earth a mix-up occurred? We'll explore how adapting your style of communication, setting the context and checking for clarity can help prevent misunderstanding and confusion.

2. The Big Argument – where a convivial start spirals out of control and into a bitter row with a partner, a family member, a work colleague, a neighbour or anyone else you had no intention of falling out with.

Throughout the book we'll examine why conversations escalate into arguments, why the subtext of the argument can be more important than the content and how you can keep things at ground level.

3. The Bad Place – where the conversation you were having with someone has gone horribly wrong and you're in the mire. Or where you simply feel disconnected and fed up with someone, and are left wondering how you're going to address the issue or recover the situation.

Getting into the Bad Place from time to time is part and parcel of any relationship, but you'd probably like to get into it less often and, when you do, be there for less time. *Watch Your Language* will show you how.

4. The Lockdown – where feelings and thoughts are internalized or withheld and negative conclusions are drawn, leading to an implosion rather than to the explosion of the Big Argument.

If someone's in the Lockdown, they'll withdraw and won't want to talk, even though it's obvious they're deeply upset. This book offers ways to restore communication and bring your relationship onto an even keel.

Through a series of accessible and easy-to-follow techniques, this book will help you to avoid the pitfalls that lead to the Tangle, the Big Argument, the Bad Place and the Lockdown. It explains how your survival instincts can hook you away from your values and reveals the warning signs that indicate when a conversation is beginning to go wrong before it's too late to turn back. And, if an interaction has already gone awry, this book will show you how to turn things around with the relationship intact.

Above all, *Watch Your Language* provides the insights and skills to enable more effective, uplifting and truly rewarding conversations.

WHAT DO I MEAN BY CONVERSATION?

Sandwiched somewhere between 'convent' and 'convoluted', a conversation is described by the *Oxford English Dictionary* as: 'A talk, especially an informal one, between two or more people, in which news and ideas are exchanged.'

Prior to the late 19th century, talk required face-to-face communication or letter-based exchanges, but the invention of the telephone changed all that. Since the advent of the internet, the way we interact has been turned upside down again and conversations can be conducted via multiple different channels, and we switch between them with little conscious effort.[1]

Conversations are central to our lives and most of us spend a staggering proportion of our waking life interacting with others. For teachers, people in customer-facing roles or managers of teams, more than 75 per cent of their day can involve communicating through one channel or another. Yet, when I ask teenagers how much time they spend at school studying the skills necessary for successful conversation, I'm met with blank looks. It's an unacknowledged issue. People may be particularly adept in their subject areas, but the progress of so many talented and intelligent individuals is constrained because their skills in conversation have never advanced beyond being merely functional.

HOW THE BOOK WORKS

Each chapter in *Watch Your Language* is short and self-contained, focusing on a specific topic with clear steps for action and a key lesson. I'd recommend reading the whole book and then returning to the chapters that you feel are most useful for you.

To make it easier to navigate your way through the different types of conversation, the book includes a cast of characters (each with his or her own icon, as shown below) in a variety of situations in which they experience conversations that go wrong. In each case, I explain how they could change the way they speak and listen to achieve a more rewarding outcome.

Dan and Beth find that conversations between them can escalate into damaging arguments. Beth is applying for a senior role at a local primary school, which involves a demanding interview process and adds to her stress levels.

Lara is full-time mother to Jack (7) and Anna (5). Her husband Ethan is Dan's elder brother and works for a bank. They have different communication styles, which often leads them into the Tangle.

Mia is a social worker and is married to Ravi, who's an IT manager. Their children are Yash (13), Ria (12) and Jay (10), each of whom presents different communication challenges. Mia used to be inseparable from her old school friend Lara, but they have drifted apart, putting a strain on their friendship.

Diane has a high-pressure job and manages a diverse team, including Beth. She is a single parent to Abby (17) and Ben (15) and treads a delicate tightrope between staying close to her teenagers and not being a pushover.

Bill lives next door to Beth and Dan and is highly opinionated. Dan tends to avoid Bill but, since he's not about to move house, needs to find ways to get on with his irritating neighbour.

Lily is Dan and Ethan's mum and was widowed two years ago. She loves seeing her extended family but she also likes her own space, and the family dynamics can become complicated.

The characters, who range in age from their 20s to their 70s, have a variety of occupations and personalities, and need to balance the demands of work with the desire to maintain happy and healthy relationships at home. The conversations quoted in *Watch Your Language* are largely adapted from accounts of real situations, as well as transcripts of actual conversations.

MY OWN JOURNEY

My understanding of the field of communication has been gleaned more through practice and making mistakes than natural talent. As an introverted 18-year-old I had the humbling experience of working in India with amputees taking their first uncertain steps toward rebuilding their shattered lives. Speaking no Hindi, my method of communication involved sign language, drinking immense quantities of tea and – much to their amusement – drawing portraits of them in my sketchbook. This set the tone for an eclectic career, during which I've been a professional artist, consultant and business owner. It's also included an underlying quest to understand the dynamics of effective communication. In the process I've been privileged to work with tens of thousands of people on every continent, ranging from leaders of large organizations to entrepreneurs, sports professionals and people living in conflict zones.

As a father I've experienced the awe and terror of having a newborn child in my arms while wondering where the manual on parenting was. In the blink of an eye, I've watched our children grow into adults and had to find new ways to communicate with them. Learning how to be a loving husband and father has been the toughest challenge I've ever faced, and by far the most rewarding.

No great artist or writer would ever dream of saying that they've learned everything there is to know about their medium. Equally, I can make no claims to mastery of conversation, but I remain infinitely curious and keen to learn and improve. When it comes to communication, we all muck things up and the ongoing challenge is ever present: can we get it right more often than we get it wrong, and can we get better at conducting the conversations that really count? The answer is a resounding yes!

WHAT TO DO?

STEP 1:
Observe Conversations

Becoming an expert starts with being curious about the dynamics of conversation. Take time to consciously step back from the content of your interactions and observe what moves them forward or brings them to a grinding halt:

- Watch how a work meeting spirals out of control if there are no pauses between speakers, and how it becomes a contest for people to get their word in.
- Become aware of the 'triggers' that propel you into defensive reactions. In these moments, you lose rational thinking and your emotions seem to take over.
- Notice when an email exchange is in danger of getting out of control and sleep on it overnight before firing off an exasperated reply.
- Recognize how your conversational style changes when you're stressed or under pressure, and whether you become directive or withdrawn. At these moments it's easy to conclude that other people are being

awkward and rude, forgetting that our own interpretations and responses may be contributing to the problem.

- Observe whether each person's voice is heard in meetings, or whether the 'share of voice' is dominated by the person who holds the most senior rank.

Daily life offers us endless opportunities to notice how a comment, pause or the lift of an eyebrow can change the direction of a conversation – for better or worse. Rather than moving blindly through your interactions, keep an observant eye on how your conversations are unfolding and an open, non-judgemental ear tuned in to the conversations people have around you.

Lesson 1: Don't just be in conversations, observe them

CHAPTER
TWO

SPOT THE SIGNS

How to Tell When a Conversation Is Going Wrong

For 99 per cent of human existence, people lived as foragers in small, tight-knit communities in which they honed their survival instincts – seeking food, shelter, protection against aggressors and a sense of belonging. When plotted against this timeline, the development of the printing press, the telephone and the internet have all happened in a micro-second. Each of them has transformed the way we speak, listen and communicate. Yet, despite embedding these technologies in societies across the globe, the human brain remains more attuned to the world of our distant ancestors than to our brave new world.

What implications does this have for the way we conduct conversations? Under pressure, our survival instincts are liable to kick in, based on elementary desires for control, certainty and self-protection. The boy who knocks over a drink and instantly blames his sister is acting on reflex, without consideration or reflection. So is the mother who shouts at her child in frustration even though she knows it will spark the Big Argument, and the work colleagues who recognize the crucial role of listening and yet can't seem to keep their mouths shut. The fact is that many of our behaviours are 'mindless' – the flip side of mindful – in the sense that they are knee-jerk responses which, on subsequent reflection, are unhelpful, ill-conceived or even untrue.[2] In these situations, we know we should think before we speak, or find our voice instead of remaining mute, or make a phone call rather than firing off an intemperate email. But, for some reason, we don't.

The truth is that instincts are tricky. We've all thanked our lucky stars after we listened to our gut and ignored the voice of reason, and yet, in equal measure, our instincts can be an unreliable compass for decision-making and lead us into perilous waters.

THE WARNING LIGHTS

Take this example when Beth and Dan have a clash of priorities. Beth enters the front room, where Dan is sitting, engrossed in the TV:

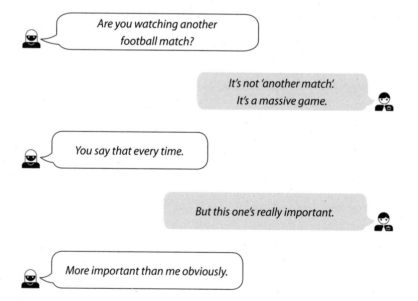

Are you watching another football match?

It's not 'another match'. It's a massive game.

You say that every time.

But this one's really important.

More important than me obviously.

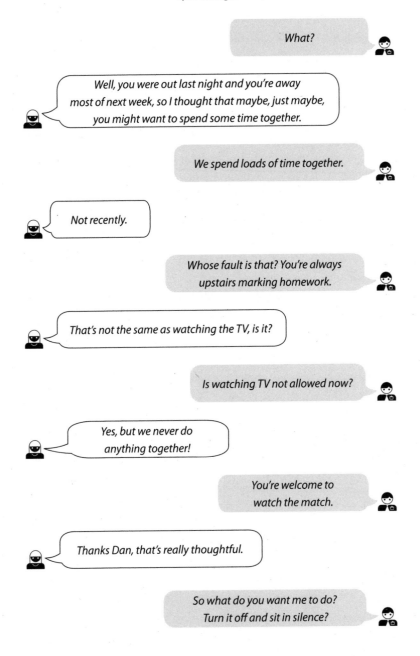

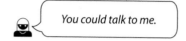

You could talk to me.

(VOICE RAISED) I am talking!!

While, in terms of its usefulness, Beth and Dan's conversation is going absolutely nowhere, it's actually heading at high speed into the Big Argument and the Bad Place. On board planes, displays of warning lights alert pilots to impending danger and protect against unseen hazards and imminent disaster. Similarly, there are warning lights that appear in our conversations. We often don't recognize them or choose to ignore them.

What are the signals that indicate Beth and Dan's interaction is heading into jeopardy? There are four primary warning lights that tell you when a conversation is going wrong. I'm not suggesting that a poor conversation is always due to one of these four things – sometimes it's a straightforward case of mixed messages – but these reactions are guaranteed to work like gunpowder in your interactions.

1. Blocking – when you are putting up your defences, because you don't want to hear what someone's saying or because they are threatening your worldview or identity.

The most obvious reason for blocking is that we don't like what we're hearing, or don't agree with it. Young children respond by sticking their fingers in their ears, and adults do the same thing, only metaphorically.

One of the most obvious ways of blocking is to withdraw our listening. We zone out what the other person's saying – a technique we mastered as children in response to pesky and controlling adults – or we employ multifarious methods of deflection. For example, whenever we say 'Yes, but…', we are employing a basic blocking technique, in which we try to reject or push away someone's words. To some extent this is a universally accepted tactic, for the simple reason that we all do it, but repeated and more extreme forms of blocking can turn into stonewalling and may have a terminal impact on a relationship when used habitually.

How can you tell when you're blocking? The person you're interacting with won't feel heard, and their voice will either increase in volume or they will withdraw from engaging with you because they don't feel they can reach you.

2. Blamestorming – when the accusations and criticisms are starting to fly, and self-righteousness is taking hold.

If a conversation's starting to turn into a blame game, with someone being accused of being at fault, it's a clear signal of blamestorming. You won't be interested in sharing responsibility, taking a balanced view or finding a pragmatic solution. You'll use language like 'they always' and 'you never', and you'll probably try to make yourself look like the innocent victim by loading the blame for an issue or problem on someone else's shoulders.

If the person you're blaming isn't the person you're having the conversation with, that person becomes an easy target because they're out of earshot and can't defend themselves. In these kinds of situations people often build on each other's comments:

'He's useless.'
'Yeah, worse than useless.'
'Tell me about it!'
… and so on.

You're closing ranks, looking for people to concur with your point of view. It's like a snowball rolling downhill, increasing in size as it goes.

Having a blamestorming conversation with someone who's in front of you is more like a boxing match. You'll start trading opinions with each other, in which the gist of the conversation is that it's the other person's fault. You may find yourself saying, 'I'm not arguing with you, I'm just explaining why you're wrong.'

How can you tell when you're blamestorming? You'll find yourself being more committed to apportioning blame than to resolving the issue.

3. Discounting – when you reject, disregard or dismiss someone's thoughts, opinions or ideas because they don't match yours, or because you want to get one-up on them.

Discounting devalues another person's idea or contribution by brushing it aside. You subtly put them down a peg or two and, in doing so, elevate your own viewpoint, status or sense of worth. Even today, decades on, I can picture the schoolteachers who made me feel ten feet tall, and the ones who made me feel small in order to elevate their own standing or self-worth. This is the power of language, for better or worse.

Discounting is one of the oldest tricks in the book and can be performed in a multitude of ways. We all do it, usually by failing to listen or saying something in a tone that diminishes another person. In response to a comment, we might say, 'I could have told you that,' inferring that we already knew what they said. While discounting is intrinsic to the push and pull of human dialogue, it can have a drip-drip effect on the quality of our relationships over time and can be devastating when used in a contemptuous manner.

How can you tell when you're discounting? The answer isn't straightforward because we tend to employ it covertly. Unless you're a politician, in which case it's an overt tool for downplaying opponents, it usually happens in the shadows of our conversations. With careful attention, we can start to distinguish whether we are lifting people up or putting them down.

4. Domineering – when a conversation's flow and rhythm starts to fall apart because you're trying to take control or drive it towards your agenda.

The most common form of domineering is to talk over another person and finish their sentences. We do this when we're trying to drive the conversation on our terms, not listening to what's being said and not allowing space for the other's opinion or disagreement.

At their best, conversations feel like a joyous and reciprocal process of turn-taking. At their worst, the story is very different: we become so invested in our opinions that the process becomes more like a wrestling match. Our attempts to control the conversation are met with resistance to control, and so it goes on.

How can you tell when you're domineering? It feels competitive – you'll notice you're interrupting the person you're speaking with and not taking time to pause, listen and reflect. The gaps between speakers will disappear, and you'll be trampling on each other's words. In these instances, winning takes precedence over making sure that the other person feels heard.

Each of these techniques has a corresponding impact on other people's experience, as follows:

- When we deploy blocking techniques, people feel unheard.
- When we engage in blamestorming, they feel criticized.
- When we are discounting, they feel undervalued.
- When we are domineering, they feel controlled.

SEEING THE SIGNALS

How do the warning lights play out in Beth and Dan's conversation?

From the start of their interaction, Dan's on the defensive. If he'd stopped and thought about it, he would have responded differently, but Beth's tone seems to trigger his survival instincts and it all happens in a split second. Suddenly the warning lights are flashing.

If Beth and Dan could recognize the signals, they could change direction before they're dragged into the Big Argument and the Bad Place.

WHAT TO DO?

STEP 1:
Notice the Warning Lights

In any area of life, warning lights are worthless if you don't notice them. They're designed to impose themselves on your consciousness. In the same way, you need to attend to the warning lights in your conversational life the moment they appear – not as an afterthought.

When you look out for them, you'll begin to notice the warning lights in your work meetings, kitchen-table discussions or conversations going on around you. Being able to spot them isn't a licence for you to point out what other people are doing wrong. For instance, if you accuse someone of blamestorming, you're likely to be doing the very same thing yourself. The warning signals act like an alert system, enabling you to make choices about how to proceed.

STEP 2:
Consider Your Choices

Coming back to Beth and Dan's argument, let's freeze it after Beth says, 'Are you watching another football match?'

Dan instinctively and automatically defends himself – this is his shotgun reaction – but he does have alternative responses available to him. For example:

- **Shotgun reaction**: He can claim that he's watching a 'massive game.' He's exaggerating, but if he makes the game seem more important, it's harder for Beth to object.
- **Alternative response**: He can say something neutral such as, 'Yeah, I was hoping to watch football, but did you have something else in mind?'

Dan's shotgun reaction requires little cognitive effort, whereas the alternative response requires stepping back, considering Beth's needs as well as his own and letting go of his attachment to watching the game.

Beth already holds the view that Dan puts his needs before hers, and his reaction cements her opinion. Her comment, 'You say that every time', is a way of signalling her displeasure, and they move into blamestorming.

Let's freeze their conversation again at the point Beth reminds Dan that he was out last night and will be away during the week. This is code for saying, 'I feel like I come last on your priority list'. Once again, Dan has options available to him:

- **Shotgun reaction**: He can say, 'You're always upstairs marking homework,' which implies that Beth works in the evenings out of choice rather than necessity, and that she's being unreasonable.
- **Alternative response**: He can say, 'You're right, let's make sure we spend time together over the weekend. Do you want to do something now, or when this is over?'

My point is that Dan's brain 'serves up' an automatic response that comes to him easily and doesn't involve him having to think or backtrack but may not be in the interests of his relationship. Here, he discounts Beth's comment about spending more time together, in order to domineer the conversation.

Ironically, if Dan opted for the alternative response, Beth would probably say, 'It's fine, we'll do something after the game's finished,' because Dan has demonstrated consideration for her. In fact, there's a double irony: Dan has hyped the significance of the game and would have been happy to switch it off if Beth had responded in a more level way. This is the absurdity and complexity of arguments – they can take us to a place that defies logic or common sense.

The warning lights are flashing, but Dan and Beth are already in the Bad Place by the time they get more perspective, by which point they are in the Lockdown.

As you engage in conversation, start to acknowledge that you have an almost infinite number of choices about how you can respond at each stage. Once you do this, the next step is to develop your skill in making the best choice in the circumstances.

Watch Your Language will enable you to recognize the opportunities open to you when you're in the heat of a difficult conversation and give you the skills to turn things around to everyone's advantage.

Lesson 2: You always have a choice about how you respond

CHAPTER
THREE

HOLD THE TRUTH LIGHTLY

How to Avoid Talking Yourself into a Drama

We can all be prone to hyperbole. You may say, 'I'm starving', if you're an hour late for lunch, or, 'I won't fit into my jeans', if you're eyeing up a piece of cake and worrying about the consequences. We often exaggerate, and use comparisons and analogies to make a point. When Lady Gaga said, 'I live halfway between reality and theatre at all times', she was speaking for all of us. We don't have a choice about the circumstances we're born into but each of us has a say in the way we interpret life and how we describe it.

If we didn't embroider the truth, life would be dull and Hollywood would be bankrupt. As the great producer Samuel Goldwyn once said, 'We want a story that starts out with an earthquake and works its way up to a climax.'[3] During our conversations it can be very tempting to intersperse the sharp facts of reality with dramatic interpretation. Problems arise when we unwittingly talk ourselves into the Bad Place.

CREATING STORIES

Take this example: the bank that Dan's high-flying brother Ethan works for is merging with another organization. The facts of the situation are:

- The new organizational structure hasn't been finalized.
- Ethan's spoken to two other people who are worried about their future.
- Depending on their position, some people will need to reapply for their jobs.
- A month ago Ethan's CEO told him, 'I think you'll be fine,' but they haven't spoken since.
- While Ethan was at work yesterday, the leadership team spent six hours in meetings.

But this is how Ethan describes it to Dan, over a couple of beers:

> *We're all in a total vacuum and everyone's fearing the worst. It even looks like we're going to have to reapply for our jobs. It's unbelievable! My CEO said he thought I'd be safe, but that was months ago and he's blanked me ever since. It looks like I'm definitely heading for the exit. What nobody realizes is that I'm keeping the business afloat while they swan about, going from one meeting to the next.*

Ethan is taking the facts that he's aware of and creating a fictional story around them. While the facts are essentially neutral, his version of the situation casts his CEO as the villain while he plays the oppressed hero. By doing this, Ethan encourages Dan to adopt his point of view and become an ally in his struggle against an adversary he's imagined.

There's nothing unique about what Ethan's doing. We all tend to follow this pattern. When we speak, we create an angle that plays to our advantage – it makes us look more heroic or more like the innocent victim. Our dramatization of events becomes a neural movie, which in turn influences our emotional state. Each time we tell our story, it becomes more concrete in our mind, to the point where we think our characterization is a statement of truth.

GETTING STUCK IN A VIEW

So what's wrong with using a little artistic licence when it comes to interpreting events? Ethan isn't being intentionally deceptive or saying anything he doesn't actually believe, but there are two repercussions that he cannot clearly see:

1. Ethan's version of events has a significant and negative influence on his own feelings. Read both the facts and Ethan's account of the situation again, and think about the emotions each might provoke. I'd argue that the facts don't incite a strong reaction, positive or negative. On the other hand, Ethan's story stirs up strong negative emotions. He feels:

   - **Angry** ('It even looks like we're going to have to reapply for our jobs. It's unbelievable!')
   - **Let down** ('My CEO said he thought I'd be safe, but that was months ago and he's blanked me ever since.')
   - **Anxious** ('It looks like I'm definitely heading for the exit.')
   - **Undervalued** ('What nobody realizes is that I'm keeping the business afloat while they swan about, going from one meeting to the next.').

The knock-on effect of Ethan's feelings is that they affect his productivity and morale at work and spill over into his home life. Jack and Anna, his young children, are noticing that he seems particularly grumpy – commenting to each other that, 'Dad seems very cross at the moment.' And his wife, Lara, is avoiding the topic of their holiday plans; she can see he's not in the right mood to listen or to think constructively.

2. Ethan's interpretation of the situation isn't true! He's not in possession of all the facts, and his perspective is one of many possible ways of looking at things. As it turns out, he's not privy to the following pieces of information:

- Some people *will* need to reapply for their jobs – where there are overlaps – but this won't apply to Ethan's area.
- The directors have agreed that Ethan will run a newly merged team.
- The leadership team has decided not to communicate the details until the whole structure is agreed.

Against the background of these additional facts, Ethan's story falls apart. He's got into the Tangle and now the Bad Place, but it's all in his head and self-created. He's compounding the problem through the way he speaks about it. He really doesn't have to be in this situation. Of course, we're rarely in possession of all the facts, and it's understandable that someone would be anxious when there's a degree of uncertainty about the future. However, if Ethan could hold the truth lightly, it would help him remain open to other interpretations of what's happening. Instead, he's reacted to his fear and anxiety, becoming narrow-minded and – to a degree – out of kilter with reality.

NEGATIVE BIAS AND FIXED POSITIONS

Our thinking tends to be negatively biased, meaning that we are more sensitized to look for what's wrong than what's right. It's actually a highly effective survival mechanism that we carry with us from the distant past. Living the forager lifestyle, our ancestors were constantly scouting the horizon for aggressors – both human and animal. If you were peering into the gloom at dusk and saw a dark shape, would you assume that it's friend or foe? Erring on the side of caution and being ready with a means of defence increased the odds of survival. As a child, before I went to sleep, I always looked to see if monsters were lurking under my bed. Even though I knew it was pretty unlikely, I still said to myself, 'Tonight might be the night!'

Under pressure, we are inclined to adopt a defensive stance in case things don't go to plan. Ethan is mentally and emotionally preparing himself for the possibility that he'll lose his job, by adopting a negative and fixed attitude. This is reflected in his blamestorming conversations. But there's a price to be paid. His stress levels are running high and his emotional state is having an impact on Lara and the children. If he could hold the truth lightly and be more flexible in his thinking, he would experience less stress.

WHAT TO DO?

STEP 1:

Manage Your Mind

When Ethan speaks to Dan, it would be more useful if he separated the facts of the situation from the stories going on in his head. Rather than saying, 'We're all in a total vacuum and everyone's thinking the worst …', he could have said, 'I've spoken to a few other people who are worried about their jobs.' And instead of saying, 'It looks like I'm definitely heading for the exit,' he could have emphasized the fact that his CEO had told him, 'I think you'll be safe,' without adding the comment about being blanked. This mental sorting process isn't instinctive and requires practice.

If Ethan can separate the facts from his interpretations, on a moment-by-moment basis, he can avoid talking himself into a drama. I'm not saying he's wrong to have interpretations; he just needs to recognize them for what they are. And, if he feels that facts are rather thin on the ground, he can probably go to someone for more information.

STEP 2:

Own Your Own Story

Imagine two people sitting opposite each other, pointing their fingers and saying, 'You always do this and never do that.' Now imagine these same two people saying, 'My story about you is that you always do this and you never do that.' The difference is that the second version balances the responsibility between the person who is supposedly at fault and the author of the story – and it's technically accurate too.

If Ethan had prefaced his account of his work situation by saying to Dan, 'This is my story about what's happening', it would have signalled to both of them that it's just that – a story. Taking this approach helps avoid falling into blamestorming.

I once worked with an organizational team whose members would say, 'You seem to be in a different story to me,' when they reached an apparent disagreement with each other. It was a reminder to loosen the grip on their own version of the truth and an invitation to explore each other's version more deeply.

> **Lesson 3: You are the author of your interpretations**

CHAPTER
FOUR

STAND CLEAR OF THE ESCALATORS

How to Prevent Trivial Conversations Becoming Toxic Arguments

The explorer Deborah Shapiro spent 15 months on the Antarctic Peninsula with her husband Rolf. Nine of these months were in complete isolation. When they returned to civilization, people wanted to know how they'd managed to avoid killing each other. They replied that, since they relied on each other for survival, murder would have been counterproductive.[4] But they did cite the example of a man killing his colleague over a chess game when stationed at a remote Antarctic station. As Shapiro pointed out, the tragedy could have started from the man not liking the way his colleague buttered his toast – and ended up in homicide.

Research shows that most arguments start as a result of trivial irritations such as leaving dirty clothes on the floor or not doing the washing-up. Starting out seemingly simple, these situations can quickly spiral to a point where the people involved are questioning their relationships.

THE SPIRAL

Escalation is what happens when we ignore the warning lights of blocking, blamestorming, discounting and domineering. When your anger takes over, you'll find yourself making wild and exaggerated claims, dragging up the past, drawing below-the-belt comparisons and making threats you're likely to regret later. When a conversation is escalating, you may find yourself saying at the top of your voice, 'Stop shouting!', to which the other person may bellow back, 'I'm not shouting!'

The stakes can get pretty high when a conversation shifts into escalation. If you fail to notice the signals you can end up cashing in all your chips as you try to win. When your stress response is activated, you develop tunnel vision, making it difficult to see the full cost of your actions until it's become destructive and you've found yourself in the Bad Place.

One Tuesday, schoolteacher Beth gets home first after work and begins preparing a meal for herself and Dan. She gets a text from Dan saying:

```
Sorry. delayed @ work. on my way. c u soon xx
```

When Dan eventually gets home, this is their conversation:

You've been ages. Your food's cold.

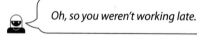

Sorry ... I had to stop for a lightning pint with Ethan. He needed some moral support.

Oh, so you weren't working late.

I was, but Ethan's having a work crisis and he collared me for a ten-minute pint.

 Ten minutes??!!

OK, it was a bit longer, but don't get this out of perspective.

 Perspective! Your text said you were at work. I'd call that a lie!

Beth, you're going overboard. I haven't slept with anyone … I JUST HAD A BEER!

 It's NOT ABOUT THE BEER! You lied about where you were. I'm not going to be in a relationship where we lie to each other!

Now you're hysterical. Next time I'll stay in the pub. I bet Ethan doesn't have this kind of grief when he gets home.

 And I bet he's not a liar either.

(She leaves the room, slamming the door.)

In less than a minute, Dan and Beth are in the Bad Place. Each comment has taken the intensity and volume of their argument to another level, blowing the lid off the conversation. Afterwards they feel angry, misunderstood, bewildered and – for a while at least – right about their point of view.

WHAT WAS THAT ABOUT?

Comparing what happened to the launch of an Apollo rocket can help us get to the bottom of Dan and Beth's exchange. Just like their argument, the rocket that put the first man on the moon reached maximum velocity in a number of stages. Burning vast quantities of kerosene and liquid oxygen, the engines fired the rocket 42 miles into the sky in less than three minutes, whereupon its first-stage engines dropped away and its second-stage ones shot it into space. Finally, as it hurtled out of the earth's atmosphere, the third-stage engines took over – propelling it on its course to the moon.

Beth and Dan have gone through their own mini lift-off, which has also happened in stages:

First Stage: creating the spark for an argument – Dan was telling the truth when he said he was working late. What he didn't do was let Beth know he'd got a last-minute call from Ethan inviting him for a quick pint. If he'd told her that Ethan seemed a bit troubled and they were going for a drink, she probably would have understood and wouldn't have made the effort to cook for him. It's often the small things, which could be avoided, that ignite an argument.

Second Stage: accusations and justifications – Having stewed for an hour waiting for Dan to come home, Beth is upset and gets on the front foot as soon as the door opens. Once their survival instincts are activated, accusations and justifications create the thrust that blasts Beth and Dan into a confrontation. The more she accuses, the more he defends his position, claiming that he made a generous sacrifice for his brother and inferring that she's overreacting. Her feelings of anger intensify; the more accusing she becomes, the more hard-done-by he feels.

There is another way Dan could have reacted, meeting Beth's accusations with counter-accusations rather than a justification. It would go like this:

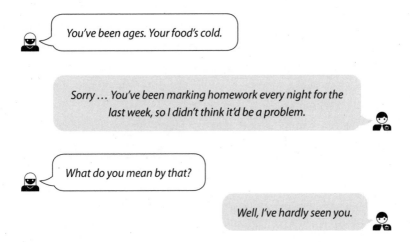

You've been ages. Your food's cold.

Sorry … You've been marking homework every night for the last week, so I didn't think it'd be a problem.

What do you mean by that?

Well, I've hardly seen you.

Here, Dan would be taking the front-foot position, diverting the conversation away from his visit to the pub and catching Beth off-guard. The result would be much the same. Accusations and justifications, or accusations and counter-accusations, are strategies we employ to win a disagreement but they also act as the fuel that allows an argument to take off, pushing it into orbit.

Neither Beth nor Dan is willing to back down or cede control, and there are no pauses in the conversation, so it becomes a battle of righteousness. Feeling they're not being heard intensifies their anger, which adds more fuel to their face-off.

Third Stage: comparisons and threats – As an argument gets further and further off the ground it reaches a point where courtesy, consideration and good manners are totally abandoned and people simply let rip. Beth and Dan reach this point when they move into comparisons and threats.

First, in an attempt to make Beth feel as if she's being over the top, Dan downplays his misdemeanour by comparing it to sleeping with someone. Seeing through his tactic, and riled by it, Beth opts for a threat. When she says, 'I'm not going to be in a relationship where we lie to each other!', she clearly means, 'I don't want to be in a relationship where you lie to me!' Stung by this, Dan makes a comparison with Lara, which he knows will get through Beth's defences. Beth's parting shot and the slammed door announce that the argument has reached its climax, and they find separate places to seethe and eventually cool down.

It's important to remember that arguments are a healthy part of any relationship, but when they get out of control they can become destructive, at least if they're not cleared up effectively. Beth and Dan never meant their argument to get so vitriolic. At times the process of escalation accelerates at breakneck speed and without any mindful consideration of what's happening and where it's going. It's a verbal scrap in which all sorts of tricks come into play, with threat being your ace. You get so focused on winning the argument that you lose situational awareness and don't notice the damage and hurt you may be causing – until it's too late.

WHAT TO DO?

STEP 1:

Keep Your Conversations at Ground Level
Here are three things Dan could have done to avoid him and Beth ending up in the Bad Place. Try them if you find yourself in a similar situation.

1. He could have **listened to Beth without interrupting**, even if she had a lot to say.

> *I'm exhausted; I had a full-on day … I went shopping on the way home, then cooked a meal … and I had absolutely no idea that you were off for a pint with Ethan … you didn't even bother to call!*

When you disagree with someone, the tendency is to interject. Listening without interruption is counterintuitive but becomes easier with practice. It would have slowed down the pace and intensity of their conversation and made Beth feel that she was being listened to.

2. Dan could have **acknowledged Beth's feelings and empathized with her**. If he'd done so, with absolutely no sarcasm in his voice, it could have had a remarkable effect on the situation. When a conversation escalates, both parties start feeling anger in one form or another – irritation, annoyance or frustration. If feelings aren't being heard or acknowledged, they increase in intensity. If he'd acknowledged her feelings, Beth wouldn't have needed to escalate them.

> *You cooked for us both … then had to eat alone while my dinner went cold … plus you couldn't reach me … it's wrecked your evening.*

3. He could have **called to let Beth know what he was doing** before going to the pub. If he'd done this, he could have reframed her expectations and avoided subsequent problems. Even if he hadn't, Dan could have got the conversation back to ground level after coming home, by thanking Beth for preparing a meal and apologizing for being inconsiderate. There's every chance she would have accepted this, so long as he made no attempt to prove his innocence or shift the blame on to her.

> *I'm really sorry, Beth. I just didn't think. I should have called you after Ethan rang, before I left the office. Thanks for cooking for me.*

STEP 2:
Press STOP!

Putting a conversation on hold is easier than you might think. Without making it an Oscar-winning exit, create some distance from the conversation by removing yourself physically from it – even for a moment or two. It'll give you some crucial thinking time and help you regain your centre of gravity.

If you're in a work meeting, make whatever excuse seems appropriate to leave the room for a few minutes. If you're at home, you may have to be more insistent about needing your own space because the person you're talking to may not want to stop. Beth could have tackled it this way with Dan:

 > *I need to take some time out from this conversation before it gets worse.*

> *Hang on a minute. You can't back out now.*

 > *Sorry, I'm feeling really upset. I need to stop this and come back to it later.*

It may feel uncomfortable, but it acts like a firebreak, helping to defuse the confrontation and prevent it from becoming destructive.

STEP 3:
Listen to What You're Saying

Exaggerations, accusations, comparisons and threats all lead to escalation. If you notice that they're being used in a conversation, it's time to bring it back to ground level. Being aware of what's happening in a conversation gives you the chance to steer a different course.

I am reminded of a quote by Stephen R. Covey, attributed to the great Viktor Frankl who survived the Holocaust but suffered the destruction of his family in the Nazi concentration camps: 'Between stimulus and response, there is a space. In that space lies our freedom to choose a response. In our response lies our growth and our freedom.'[5]

In the same way, we can choose how we respond in a conversation, even when our emotions are running high.

Lesson 4: Arguments don't 'just happen'

CHAPTER
FIVE

IDENTIFY
THE SUBTEXT

How to Decipher What People Really Mean When They Speak

Some conversations can be bewildering. You can be sitting three feet away from someone and feel as though you're on a different planet. The Tangle isn't just the result of people not listening to each other. It also happens when there's a mismatch between what people think and what they say. Often the real action is happening in the sub-plot of a conversation, hidden from view.

I once had a row with my wife, Sally, when a family friend was staying. We started quarrelling about what soup to cook for lunch, then about how much everyone would want. After a couple of minutes our friend cut across our arguing, 'You do realize this argument isn't about the soup, don't you?'

Her comment stopped us in our tracks. She was right. Our minor irritations with each other had spilled into our conversation about lunch. It's a fact; most arguments are *not about the issue you're talking about,* making it difficult to resolve the disagreement – you're actually having the wrong conversation. Sally and I were never going to sort out our frustrations with each other while we stayed on the subject of soup.

In most arguments, the real issues lie below the surface, either unseen or unacknowledged. One of the secrets of being a conversation expert is the ability to get better at identifying and addressing the subtext of a conversation before it starts heading toward the Tangle, the Big Argument or the Bad Place.

It's important to make a distinction between the content of a conversation – the words that are actually being spoken – and the subtext. Often, what's happening beneath the surface is running the show.

AIR FLORIDA FLIGHT 90

Failing to understand subtext can have disastrous consequences. Look at the following extracts from the black box recording of a domestic passenger flight that crashed into the Potomac River outside Washington DC, leading to the deaths of 78 people.[6] Having been delayed for one hour and 45 minutes due to a snowstorm and temperatures of -4°C, the first officer of Air Florida Flight 90 had concerns that the plane shouldn't take off, but the captain was focused on getting airborne. The following dialogue shows what they said to each other, and the lightly shaded boxes indicate what the first officer might have been thinking:

See all those icicles on the back there and everything?

I'm concerned about these icicles.

Yeah.

Boy … this is a losing battle here on trying to de-ice those things, it [gives] you a false feeling of security, that's all it does.

I'm not 100 per cent happy about this.

Let's check those tops again since we been sitting here a while.

This situation feels highly dangerous.

(In reference to instrument readings)

That doesn't seem right, does it?
Ah, that's not right.

I think we should abort take-off.

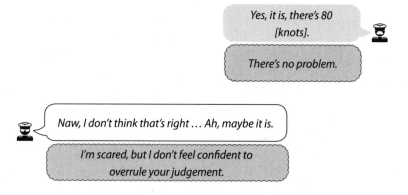

Yes, it is, there's 80 [knots].

There's no problem.

Naw, I don't think that's right ... Ah, maybe it is.

I'm scared, but I don't feel confident to overrule your judgement.

The first officer left multiple clues that he was concerned about the inclement weather, but the captain didn't pick up on them.

Why didn't the first officer say, 'STOP THE FLIGHT!'? The conclusion of the post-crash investigation was that he held back because of an unconscious belief that *first officers don't tell captains what to do*. He lacked psychological safety, which is to say that he didn't feel able to challenge the authority of his superior. As a result, he implied his concerns without making them explicit. Linguists refer to this as 'mitigated speech'.

Both of them skirted around the conversation that needed to happen to avoid the disaster. The subsequent investigation became a turning point for the aviation industry, prompting an overhaul in the way pilots were trained to communicate with each other.

Sadly, every industry has suffered tragedies for similar reasons. At 7.30am on 1st October 2015, the captain of a 791-foot-long cargo ship called *El Faro* made a distress call to say that the ship was listing while on its way to the island of Puerto Rico. Twenty minutes later the ship sank in tempestuous seas, prompting disbelief that it could have sailed directly into the path of a hurricane with the loss of 33 lives.[7]

Like the first officer of Air Florida Flight 90, it turned out that the chief mate and second mate on board the vessel were convinced that the ship should turn around, but didn't feel they had permission to question the captain's decisions.

Earlier in the voyage, the chief mate stated that he was 'anxious' to see the latest weather report, but this didn't ring any alarm bells in the mind of the captain who said in response, 'Well, we'll see how it goes.'

Later on, in the face of ferocious seas, the second mate made a call to the captain, who was slumbering in his cabin, in which she avoided making a direct request to turn the ship around but alluded to her concerns by using phrases such as, 'We'll be meeting the storm' and 'It isn't looking good right now.' Her approach was hesitant, but the subtext of her language was laden with fear, if only the captain could decode it.

HOW DO YOU CRACK THE CODE?

There's a story of an African tribal chief whose communication skills were legendary across the land. A young man from a neighbouring district went to one of his tribal meetings, determined to learn from his skills. He noticed that each time a villager asked a question the chief answered it in a way that the young man hadn't at all anticipated. Each time the questioner sat down seemingly satisfied with the chief's answer.

The young man waited until the meeting was over before approaching the chief. 'Your Highness, what is the secret behind your answers to these people's questions?' he asked.

'I don't answer the question,' the chief replied. 'I answer what gives rise to the question.'

We tend to get caught up in the content of a conversation because it's easier to address. Responding to what people say can be hard enough without trying to figure out what they're not saying. But whether a conversation is happening in the bedroom, the boardroom or the cockpit of a plane, we'd benefit from increasing our ability to decode the subtext.

During the Second World War the British government recruited a team of mathematical wizards as code breakers. They developed the Colossus, a huge computer-like machine that filled an entire room, and used it to decipher encoded messages being sent from the German Lorenz

45

machine. The Colossus was capable of reading intercepted messages at the rate of 5,000 characters per second.[8] You may think you need your own Colossus machine to work out what's happening in the subtext of a conversation. Fortunately that's not necessary, even though getting beneath the surface of what's being said is not always easy.

Lara has an old friend from university called Mia whose style of communication is very different to that of her husband, Ravi. He's more reflective than Mia, tending to keep his thoughts and concerns to himself until he's mentally processed them. This has a knock-on effect for her because, although she can tell he's unhappy about something, she doesn't necessarily know what's troubling him. There are times when she feels she's not getting anywhere.

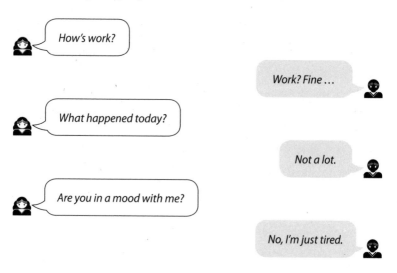

How's work?

Work? Fine …

What happened today?

Not a lot.

Are you in a mood with me?

No, I'm just tired.

Ravi's monosyllabic responses could either encourage Mia to change the subject or wind her up to the point where she starts feeling frustrated and accuses Ravi of stonewalling, which will make him withdraw even further. It's easy to see how a conversation like this could go from the Tangle to the Big Argument and finally end up in the Bad Place.

Being able to decode the subtext can stop that from happening.

WHAT TO DO?

STEP 1:
Ask Questions to Identify the Subtext and Listen

Mia assumes Ravi's in a mood with her. If she asks questions that encourage Ravi to give a deeper response, she's likely to make more progress.

> How are you feeling about work? I've noticed you've stopped talking about it recently and you seem really flat when you come home.

> It's a bit rubbish, but nothing I can't deal with.

> What's rubbish?

> Well, Steve [Ravi's boss] is being a bit of a pain.

> Oh, OK, so what's happening with Steve? What's he doing?

> He seems to be sidelining me. He used to ask for my advice all the time, but now he's always in meetings with Chris. I don't know why things have changed and I don't know what they're planning.

> And how does that make you feel?

> Ah [pauses]... I guess I feel undervalued. And annoyed. It was fine until the start of the project, and then...

Decoding the subtext of a conversation is a process. Rather than stopping after her first question, Mia goes on asking questions that reflect what Ravi's just said – while listening and being totally supportive. Instead of prompting a binary 'yes' or 'no' answer, each question invites Ravi to go a bit deeper.

If you follow through like this you can usually get below the surface to the real issue, without making the other person back off. You'll probably find they appreciate the chance to feel heard and move forward by talking things through.

Throughout their conversation Mia avoids making judgements or offering her opinion. If she'd done this, it would have broken the thread and interrupted Ravi's flow.

The questions you ask, and the way in which you ask them, will vary depending on the context, but the principle is the same: seek deeper responses, following through with a line of questions that reflect what you're hearing.

If you ask a monosyllabic teenager, 'How's school?', you're likely to end up with a one-word answer. But if you use this as an opener and then follow through with questions that encourage them to share their thoughts and feelings, you'll open the door for them to express themselves more deeply.

You can use the same principle of curiosity and inquiry when trying to decode the subtext of any conversation.

STEP 2:

Communicate Your Own Subtext

Lara is fighting a losing battle to get Jack and Anna, her children, to keep their rooms tidy. She's fed up with feeling as if she's their maid and her usual response tends to be along the lines of:

You never pick your clothes up off the floor!
Both of you – you're bone idle!

Lara's not saying what she really feels and, rather than achieving anything constructive, her response is more likely to put her children on the defensive because it's accusatory. It's also unlikely that she'd be able to justify her use of the word 'never' if Jack or Anna challenged her on it.

Lara needs to identify and name her emotions, bringing them into the foreground of the conversation. It would also be better if she spoke to Jack and Anna separately.

 I feel cross and ignored when you leave your clothes on the floor after I've asked you to pick them up. Please can you put them away this evening?

To her surprise, Lara finds that both Jack and Anna tidy their clothes of their own accord before going to bed. She realizes that she'll have to nudge them again a week – or even a day – later, but why has this worked so effectively?

Jack and Anna's proactive response is not down to luck. Firstly, Lara has dropped the recriminations and name-calling in favour of describing the impact of Jack and Anna's behaviour on the way she feels. The importance of this point cannot be understated – her children can contest her opinion until the world freezes over, but they can't argue with how she's feeling. If she says she feels cross and ignored, it would be ridiculous for them to insist that she's not.

What's more, Lara has made a clear request, without preaching, hectoring or pulling rank. Children, like adults, are fantastically attuned to attempts to control them. By not speaking down to Jack and Anna, and discounting them, Lara is equalizing the relationship and getting alongside them.

Parenting can often feel like a relentless war of attrition and Lara is well aware that the joy of having young children can be lost in a maelstrom of nagging and haggling. But this small act of responsibility on behalf of Jack and Anna brings a ray of sunshine to her evening and, when repeated to the point of becoming a habit, creates a more cooperative relationship with them.

You may not want to reveal your own subtext if you're engaged in the tricky dynamics of political negotiation or professional poker, but communicating your subtext can deepen your sense of connection with people and reduce the likelihood of mixed messages – it's another simple secret to having fulfilling conversations.

STEP 3:
Start Paying Attention to What People Aren't Saying

How do you know when there's a subtext to what someone's saying in a conversation? It's not an exact science, but if you use your intuition and pay attention to what the person may be thinking or feeling, rather than merely focusing on what they're saying, you can pick up some pretty strong clues.

If a sales manager says, 'We're behind on our numbers and there'll be hell to pay if we don't catch up,' she might actually mean, 'I'm feeling under pressure to hit my target.'

Or, if a child says, 'I don't really want to audition for the school play,' he might actually mean, 'I'm worried that I'm not good enough and I don't want to look like an idiot.'

If someone seems unusually defensive or says something out of character, it's likely there's more to what they're saying than they're letting on. Using the same technique of inquiry introduced in Step 1 can help you uncover what it is. Knowing that conversations have different layers of meaning, and being able to get beneath the surface to identify them, will help you understand the subtext better.

As they talk, people display all kinds of clues that point to what they really mean. Their intonation and body language, the ease – or otherwise – with which they're expressing themselves, the words they choose and the gaps and the silences they leave can all indicate how they're feeling.

This reminds me of the story of a doctor who received the notes on a new patient. The previous doctor's last entry was:

'Pain in neck. Has. Is.' [9]

It's easy to figure out the previous doctor's opinion of their patient. The humour is in the subtext.

STEP 4:
Be Aware of Cultural Differences

When Mia and Ravi first got together, it took a while for Mia to become familiar with his family's customs. When his Indian parents nodded their heads, she initially took this as a sign of agreement but it didn't mean they were saying 'yes'; it meant, 'I'm listening to you.' They were offering empathy, but not necessarily approval or support.

Beth also had a lesson in cultural differences while on a six-month placement, teaching English in Shanghai. She was amazed at how highly she was regarded by her Chinese pupils and their parents; much more so than in the UK. However, whenever she and the headteacher met parents together, she felt offended that the parents seemed to ignore her. Eventually she understood that the headteacher's grey hair and greater experience meant that the parents listened more keenly to his words than to hers.

Once, during a conversation that Beth had with the parents of a student, the husband appeared to disagree with his wife. Beth noticed an involuntary reaction from her – she looked as though she'd just received an electric shock. Her Chinese friends explained afterwards what had happened. The concept of 'face' is very important in their society and is inextricably linked to one's standing and worth. The husband had displayed a lack of respect for his wife by disagreeing with her in public. In doing so, she had lost face, causing him to lose face too.

Beth's experience taught her that there are countless different cultural nuances that can appear in the subtext of a conversation, shaping people's behaviour. The best way of understanding these nuances is to ask for them to be explained to you.

Lesson 5: The issue you're discussing may not be the real issue

CHAPTER
SIX

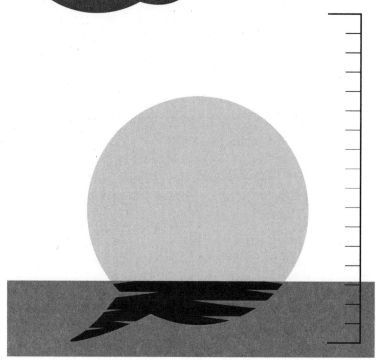

LISTEN DEEPLY

Why Shallow Listening Leads
to Shallow Relationships

There's a peculiar practice called a filibuster that's sometimes used in parliamentary proceedings. It involves a member prolonging a debate to prevent a particular vote being held. It's basically a time-wasting technique that was used back in ancient Rome and has been exemplified in more recent times by two US senators.

In 1935 the Louisiana Democrat Huey Long spent over 15 hours telling stories about his uncle and explaining how to fry oysters while his fellow senators snored, buried themselves in a good novel or caught up on their admin.[10] Long later commented that he'd been 'in heaven discussing this thing', but his fellow senators disagreed; the whole process was purgatory for them. When the call of nature finally compelled Long to dash to the men's room at 4am, his colleagues scurried into action and passed the bill he'd been trying to block.

Long's feat was topped by Strom Thurmond who, in 1957, managed to extend a monologue from 8.54pm on 28 August until 9.12pm on 29 August, all the while snacking on supplies of bread and sirloin steak. Thurmond became a legend, not because of his skills in oratory, but due to his unparalleled bladder control.

The word 'filibuster' has its roots in the Spanish word for 'freebooter' or 'pirate' – a filibuster is essentially a robber. We've all sat through lessons, lectures or meetings where it has felt as though we're enduring a Huey Long filibuster and are being robbed of time. Someone's speaking but nobody's listening.

I've experienced numerous youth football matches where the opposing team's coach has delivered a filibuster-type speech that lasts from kick-off until the final whistle. The players on his team invariably ignore him. Similarly, it's all too easy for parents to broadcast instructions without regard for whether or not they're being listened to.

However well intended, what we might think of as being helpful advice can sound like a stream of white noise.

THE SPECTRUM OF LISTENING

Often, the problem stems from conversational traffic being one-way only. Conversation is designed to be reciprocal, so being 'talked at' is antithetical to its founding principle. In short, speaking is worth nothing if we don't feel heard.

The act of listening can be a tricky thing to define, but let's create a spectrum, from shallow and functional, to deep and profound.

1. Inauthentic listening – Some people make it perfectly clear when they have no interest in what you're saying. They speak over you, change topic or openly display their irritation, which are forms of blocking or domineering. However, most of us take a stealth-based approach, in which we zone out while pretending that we're still dialled in.

I can nod my head at the right moments to make you think I'm listening, while I'm thinking about anything from dinner this evening to how I'm going to handle my next meeting. My pretence might fall apart if you ask me to repeat what you've just said, or if you seek my opinion on the matter, but even then I can ask you to clarify your last point and buy myself time to tune in. The art of pretending to listen without actually listening can be a useful device, and we all resort to it, but it's not conducive to healthy conversation.

In a similar vein, have you ever met someone for the first time whose name you struggled to remember moments after your introduction? They told you their name and you told them yours. As you shook hands, saying 'good to meet you', you could have sworn you heard what they said, but now you can't remember whether they're Ava, Leah or Luna.

You were physically there, but you weren't present, and there are numerous occasions when our attention is occupied elsewhere. In these moments of distraction, there's minimal listening going on in the conversational equation.

2. Self-referential listening – A man meets a woman at a party and they strike up a conversation. Whenever it starts to wander off in another direction the man brings it back to himself. Toward the end of the evening he says, 'Listen, I'm really sorry, I've spent the whole time talking about me. Let's talk about you.' The woman breathes a sigh of relief. 'So,' he continues, 'what do *you* think about *me*?'

This little story is a perfect example of self-referential listening. We all do it. In her book *Talk*, linguist Elizabeth Stokoe refers to the process of turn-taking as a 'conversational racetrack'.[11] We love to steer conversations onto our own track so we can share our experience, offer our opinions or prove a point. When two or more people are in this mode, the conversation's flow and rhythm will be disrupted, and the 'domineering' warning light will flash.

We like to think that conversations consist of one person speaking and the other person listening. However, the reality is a bit different. Let's take the example of Ravi and Mia, who are having a conversation about their plans for the weekend. It's not an argument, but they interrupt and finish one another's sentences in order to bring the conversation back onto their track.

While Ravi is speaking, Mia is preparing to speak. Then Mia cuts in and becomes the speaker while Ravi prepares to speak. The process continues in this way, begging the question, 'Who is doing the listening?'

My point is this: preparing to speak is not the same as listening. Of course, Ravi and Mia are both listening to a degree but, if repeated often enough, shallow listening reaps shallow relationships.

3. Pre-conceived listening – Some estimates claim that the human brain can take in 11 million bits of information a second. Whatever the truth, the point remains the same: there is a universe of difference between what we can register and what we can process. To analyze that amount of data, the human brain would need to be so large that our spine wouldn't be able to support the weight of it.

A brilliant solution is to rely on stored perceptions of the world, so the brain doesn't have to constantly re-evaluate them. Think of it like a cache system on a computer: by storing frequently used data, the computer can retrieve information more quickly, without searching for it afresh.

Unfortunately, there's a downside to this solution. We end up listening from a past-based, pre-formed perspective, and find that we're unable to listen in the here and now.

A friend told me a poignant story that illustrates this. Whenever his teenage son wanted to borrow money from him he'd say, 'Dad …?' with a similar tone, in a particular way. It got so familiar that he immediately knew that a request for money was going to follow – or so he thought. On one occasion, when his son approached him in the same way, the dad frowned and rolled his eyes. Straight away, his son muttered, 'Forget it,' and slunk off. Later that evening, the father had the presence of mind to ask his son what he'd been about to say. His reply was, 'I wanted you to know that I'd had a rubbish day at school.'

How much of life do we miss because we're busy confirming the subjective perceptions that we've established as points of view? It's much easier to confirm our opinion than to question it – especially with the people closest to us.

Listening through our preconceptions allows us to have discussion, but nothing more. The root of the word 'discussion' aptly means 'to smash apart, scatter or disperse', and the majority of our interactions conform to this definition. A supposedly straightforward topic becomes frustratingly hard and complicated, seeming to involve a repetitive process of breaking up and piecing back together again.

If we imagine the act of listening as the potential to immerse ourselves in a vast ocean, I'd argue that we generally tend to paddle up to our ankles. This is fine at a transactional level but there's a price to pay if we consistently listen in this way.

If you always remain in the shallows with those you're close to, they probably won't bother to bring up issues for fear of being judged rather than heard. And your partner won't voice any deeper concerns about your relationship for fear it'll spark yet another damaging row. These are exactly the situations in which it's vital to wade out into that ocean and listen deeply. A 2021 Prince's Trust survey found that 56 per cent of young adults in the UK aged 16 to 25 'always or often feel anxious'.[12] Against this backdrop, feeling heard is a life-support mechanism for managing their mental health.

4. Presence – There's a much deeper reservoir of listening available to us, if only we could tap into it, which requires surrendering our own needs and desires, and putting ourselves in other people's worlds. This requires being fully present while the other person's speaking and it's not as easy as it sounds because we tend to preoccupy ourselves with:

- composing a brilliant reply.
- seeking to gain the upper hand.

- evaluating the merit of what the other person's saying.
- working out how to fix the problem that's being outlined to us.
- waiting for the other person to stop speaking so that we can offer our wisdom or change the subject.

Listening from nothing is very different from listening through your agenda. It requires giving your complete attention to someone else's words, and to their world, as a precursor to speaking yourself. When you do this, you're more likely to pick up both the content of the conversation and the emotions and values in its subtext. You'll be absorbed in the present moment rather than extrapolating ahead or rewinding your mental tape. Your responses will be more agile, sharper and attuned to the other person's perspective.

Being on the receiving end of this type of listening is magical. You'll feel heard, but also deeply connected to the person who is doing the listening. Rather than telling them your thoughts and feelings, you'll feel as if you're participating together in a shared experience. Depending on who you're talking to, feelings of respect, profound affinity or love will be a natural consequence.

I was chatting about this approach to listening with a team of senior managers in South Africa. One of them, Philip, reflected on his own experience. He described the way his wife welcomed local kids and teenagers to their house. Philip had asked one of the teenagers why he chose to hang around at his place, instead of down at the football pitch with his peers. The boy replied, 'I come to your house because your wife listens *as if I'm here'.*

It's worth reading that sentence several times. Personally, I'd benefit from keeping it in mind every day. It's got a haunting quality that nags at my conscience, and I can't help scanning through a mental list of my own friends and family – wondering how well I measure up.

When people reflect on the times they've grown and flourished in their lives, they consistently report that a family member, colleague or friend 'listened as if they were there'. As the years have passed, I've concluded that this is one of the most critical legacies I'd wish to leave for my children. I'm aware that it can't be bought with money or favours. Instead, it will be the product of the many thousands of interactions I've had with them. However well I think I may have listened, they will be the judges of my success. When it comes to listening, we are all learners.

WHAT TO DO?

STEP 1:
Be in the Conversation You're in
Our modern world constantly demands that we pedal faster but effective conversation requires slowing down for long enough to be present. The truth is that we can only ever be in the conversation that we're in.

Just as a sports professional will never play to her highest potential in every match, it's impossible to be completely engaged in every interaction, but constant practice will enable you to demonstrate it more reliably. As you switch from one interaction to the next, make a conscious choice to give it your complete attention, surrendering to the present moment.

STEP 2:
Bring Your Attention Back When It Drifts
When you start listening more attentively, you'll become acutely conscious that your thoughts keep interfering. It tends to work in the following way.

Mia and Ravi are discussing their son's teacher at school. Ravi's reply of 'Um, okay then' masks the chatter in his head which is going something like this:

> *Yes … fair enough … what time is it? I've got to reply to that email by 5 o'clock … OK, I've got your point … I forgot to call the electrician yesterday … I wonder who that missed call was from …*

Ravi experiences a constant stream of mind chatter that is either past-based ('I forgot to call the electrician yesterday') or future-based ('I've got to reply to that email by 5 o'clock'). There are times when this running commentary seems to swamp his consciousness and he can't switch it off. The best he can aim for is to keep noticing when his attention drifts away and to bring it back to the conversation he's in. If he can do this more consistently, the quality of his interactions will go up exponentially.

Try practising this in every single conversation you have, every day. And, if you don't have the headspace to do it, you have the option to say, 'I'm really sorry, can we talk about this later when I have the headspace to listen to you properly?' It's more respectful and effective than casually going through the motions.

STEP 3:
Allow Pauses

Gaps and pauses during a conversation can feel uncomfortable. Our inclination is to fill them, even if it means talking drivel. Moving away from the shores of shallow listening into the depths requires giving people space to finish a sentence and inserting a pause for them to hear, in their own mind, what they've just said. I never cease to marvel at the difference this can make.

Someone might say, 'There's absolutely nothing I can do about my situation at work.' If I remember to hold back and not jump in at the end of their sentence, after a few moments of silence they may continue: 'Well, of course, that's not entirely true … I could look for another job … Or I suppose I could speak to my manager … I'm not sure he'll listen … Then again, I don't have much to lose if it goes wrong …' These moments of silence allow people to voice their deeper feelings and concerns, and reach their own solutions.

Perhaps the greatest contribution you can provide is to be fully present; allowing the person you're speaking with the time and space to become clear about how they feel, what they really think and how they wish to move forward. Sometimes the real action in a conversation takes place in the pauses, when nothing at all is being said.

Lesson 6: Listen as if the quality of your relationships depends on it

CHAPTER
SEVEN

LEAN INTO YOUR THOUGHTS AND FEELINGS

How to Deal with Negative Thoughts and Feelings

An American woman known only as SM has changed our understanding of the human brain for an unusual reason: she cannot feel fear. She suffers from a rare genetic condition called Urbach-Wiethe disease, which has destroyed her amygdala, a part of the limbic system in her brain that processes emotions. She has been held at knifepoint and gunpoint in the local precincts of her hometown in Kentucky without registering the slightest fear at all. One day her son was aghast to see her pick up a large snake on the road and place it casually in the grass so it could continue on its slithery way. Prior to her disease, she would have been freaked out by the snake – in fact, she'll still tell you today that she can't stand them – but damage to her amygdala has broken the connection between seeing danger and experiencing the moment of terror that triggers the body to recoil from it.[13]

When faced with scary situations such as public speaking or an intimidating work interview, the idea of having no fear sounds appealing, but the story of SM highlights the central role that emotions play in our daily life – telling us what we care about, warning us of impending danger, and helping us to make even the most mundane decisions.

Over the last four hundred years, no phrase has influenced the arc of western civilization more strongly than 'cogito ergo sum', which translates as 'I think, therefore I am'. This assertion was made by philosopher and mathematician René Descartes, who was the equivalent of a modern rock star in French 17th-century intellectual circles. To paraphrase, Descartes managed to put rational thinking on an almighty pedestal and diminish the status of emotions.

Today's neuroscientists are telling a different story. Without emotions, they say, decision-making becomes laborious and practically impossible. In his book *Descartes' Error*, neurobiologist Dr Antonio Damasio states that, 'We are not thinking machines, we are feeling machines that think.'[14] If Descartes could hear, he would file for libel.

I WOULDN'T BE WITHOUT IT

Thoughts and feelings come and go and it's up to us to distinguish which ones we pay attention to. Dame Judi Dench has received one Oscar, two Golden Globes and 11 BAFTA awards. Such was the force of her performance in the film *Shakespeare in Love* that she won her Oscar despite being onscreen for only nine minutes. And yet she claims that the more she acts, the more frightened she becomes. How can this be?

In contrast to thousands of aspiring performers across the world who are waiting for the day when they'll overcome their fear, Dame Judi sees her fear as being vital to her success. She understands that the battle to suppress or banish negative feelings simply can't be won. 'I have the fear,' she says. 'I wouldn't be without it.' She's made her fear more of a companion than an enemy.

ALLOWING THOUGHTS AND FEELINGS

On the subject of public speaking, I met a man called George who arrived at the same realization as Judi Dench and it transformed his life. George grew up with an absolute fear of speaking in front of large groups. Even in work meetings, with a dozen-or-so people, he'd keep his thoughts to himself. Over the years, he'd become involved in trade union organizations and was a regular attendee at their conferences. At one particular meeting, which had about 4,000 attendees, the woman leading it asked George if he'd deliver the closing speech on the following day. The idea seemed absurd to him. More than absurd – George felt physically sick at the thought.

However, the woman was very convincing. She pointed out to George that she was accountable for the success of the conference, and that she trusted him implicitly. She told him that he had something valuable to contribute. George knew this much was true.

After a lengthy conversation, and to his own astonishment, he agreed to do it. He woke during the early hours of the following day in a panic. His negative thoughts were on the rampage, telling him, 'George, this is the greatest mistake you have ever made in your life. You're going to make a complete fool of yourself. Today will ruin your career, and your reputation will be on the scrapheap.'

But George didn't want to let his friend down. He had agreed to make the closing speech, and his friend was relying on him. Before the time came, he went for a long walk along the pier, breathing in the fresh sea air and gathering himself before walking into the conference hall and delivering his speech. As he finished, 4,000 people stood up to give him a standing ovation. He now speaks at conferences the world over.

What happened? George realized that he could have all his negative thoughts and feelings and still get up and speak – just as Judi Dench can feel terrified and still deliver award-winning performances. This has significant implications if we apply it across all areas of life. It means we can be fearful and speak up, or be anxious about challenging someone and raise our concerns. Above all, it shows that we can own our thoughts and feelings rather than being owned by them.

GET BACK TO CHOICE

George's story echoes my own. As a young boy who lived away from home at an early age, I concluded that I couldn't confide my true feelings to anyone and had to stuff them into a dark corner of my being.

However, this strategy was relatively unsuccessful. I suppressed my emotions at times when I would have benefited from expressing them, but they'd spill out precisely when I wanted to shut the lid on them. The more I fought them, the more they tightened their grip on me.

As for being a teenager, I can recall being in social situations and wishing that I was invisible. Often I'd be racked with self-reproach afterwards; if only I could express my voice with freedom and assurance. When I felt especially self-conscious, my face would go a deep shade of red.

The more I sought to avoid this happening, the more it seemed to occur, proving that 'what you resist persists'. It was only when I was in my early 20s that I realized it's possible to feel embarrassed *and* still participate fully in an interaction – that they aren't mutually exclusive. The turning point for me was a conversation in which I went bright red and said, 'I'm blushing but it will pass in a minute or two', and we carried on as if nothing had happened. It was a moment of liberation and my dread of embarrassment seemed to drop away.

It would seem extraordinary to my teenage persona that I've spent the majority of my adult life speaking in public forums. On the occasions when this has involved talking in front of hundreds of people my nerves are the same – I've just learned to accept them. Since the physiological expressions of anxiety and excitement are largely the same, such as a raised heartbeat and sweaty palms, it's hard to know which I'm feeling. Over time, I've learned to accept that my thoughts and feelings can be highly paradoxical.

WHY WE TRIP UP

Beth learns this the hard way when she interviews for a role on the leadership team at a primary school, which requires meeting a panel of the school's governors. It's an intimidating process but everything seems to be going well until someone asks a particularly difficult question. It's a seminal moment, after which Beth's performance and prospects seem to spiral downward. On closer inspection, the trigger for Beth's problem is not the difficult question but a series of private thoughts that she treats as statements of truth, tipping her into the Bad Place.

What would you do if a teaching assistant came to you voicing concerns about a teacher's ability to keep control of the class?

Well, um … I'd want to meet with the teacher and see how they think things are going.

Are you sure? Wouldn't you want to discuss it with the head first, or observe part of a lesson before approaching the teacher directly?

Oh, yes … well, of course, I'd do that as well.

That was horrible. I totally blew it. He's going to think I'm useless now.

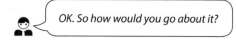

 OK. So how would you go about it?

Um, well … obviously … as you said, I'd let the headteacher know that a concern had been raised, but I'd also want to check the facts in more detail.

That was even worse. I can't believe this is happening. Now he's glaring at me.

 How exactly would you check the facts?

I'm sorry; could you repeat the question please?

Get me out of here.

After Beth notices that the governor is frowning, she has a thought that she's thrown away her chances. This thought, and *nothing more*, acts as a 'stressor' which knocks her body out of homeostatic balance and triggers a series of chemical reactions. There are two parts to the body's nervous system, which can be most easily thought of as an accelerator and a brake, and Beth's accelerator – otherwise known as the sympathetic nervous system – fires up to meet the demand of the situation.

Let's pause at this point to spare a thought for Beth. Not only is she trying to listen to what the governor is saying and formulate a vaguely intelligent response, but she's doing so against the backdrop of a tempestuous inner environment. Adrenalin (more commonly referred to nowadays as epinephrine) is coursing through her body, her heart rate is spiking and blood is being diverted towards her muscles in preparation for a fight-or-flight response.

Against the backdrop of these internal forces, it's hardly surprising that Beth is struggling to maintain her focus and has lost her centre of gravity. Ironically, the governor was rather impressed with Beth up to this point, but now her negative bias has kicked in and she's falling victim to her own self-talk. She hasn't just had a thought that she's failing the interview; she's treating it as a fact, and it sends her overall performance downhill. In a moment of intense pressure, she has forgotten that having a negative thought doesn't make it true.

Beth needs to realize that her internal dialogue can get loud and negative. She has to be able to notice it chattering away and not get tangled up in it. The challenge is the same for a professional tennis player whose game suffers because she gets caught up in thinking about the volley she missed in the last game rather than playing the point in front of her. Beth attaches significance to her thoughts and feelings and ends up getting swamped by them, rather than being able to hold the truth lightly. This dictates her mental state and subsequent responses.

What's the alternative? Ideally, Beth would have noticed her thoughts and feelings in much the same way that you might notice a cloud drifting across the sky on a breezy afternoon. When this happens, you don't grant the cloud any significance in relation to your worth and value; it doesn't make you a lesser or a greater person. Similarly, Beth could have noticed the thought:

> *That was even worse. I can't believe this is happening.*
> *Now he's glaring at me.*

To be able to do this successfully, she won't attach any significance to her thought. She'll remember that it isn't necessarily true. It'll jump into her consciousness but she'll swiftly bring her attention back into the present moment. She'll know that some of her thoughts will be positive and others intensely negative, and she'll let them come and go, while staying focused on the question being asked by the governor. In other words, her attention is outwards rather than inwards.

If Beth is able to stick to this practice under the pressure of a job interview, she'll be able to apply it across her life. When Dan, her partner, doesn't notice that she's had her hair highlighted, her negative thoughts kick in and she feels irritated. But if she's able to notice her thoughts and feelings, she doesn't have to be like a puppet on a string. Of course, this doesn't mean she can't express herself to Dan. Rather, she'll be able to stop and think about how she wants to respond instead of having a shotgun reaction which sparks the Big Argument and feels like an overreaction in hindsight.

WHAT TO DO?

STEP 1:
Notice When You're Triggered

Negative thoughts and feelings do serve a purpose. If you feel frustrated with someone, your frustration is telling you that you care about something. If you're walking home late at night and see someone who you think might be following you, your fear puts you on the alert. However, in many situations, your thoughts and feelings act as triggers, provoking an emotional reaction that hooks you away from your values.

A negative thought or feeling doesn't, in itself, prevent you from taking any action. It's easy to think, 'I'm frightened and therefore I can't speak.' This is a trick of the mind. It would be more accurate and authentic to say, 'I'm frightened and I'm choosing not to speak.' When you do so, you become the author of your decision rather than a victim of circumstance. Indeed, the greatest achievements in your life may have been accompanied by feelings of terror, concern or frustration, which you accepted as a necessary part of the process. Being triggered isn't the problem; it's what happens next that matters most.

STEP 2:
Identify Your Commitments

Having noticed your thoughts and feelings, it's worth asking yourself what you're really committed to. This will provide a more solid compass for action.

Look at the following list. Reading from left to right, what's the most reliable basis for decision-making in each situation? Is it your thoughts, your feelings or your commitments?

THOUGHTS	FEELINGS	COMMITMENTS
I can't raise the issue. It will wreck our relationship	Anxiety	To have an open and honest relationship
I'm going to hit a bad note and look like a loser	Fear	To play in the orchestra to the best of my ability
I'm never going to pass my exam. It's hopeless	Resignation	To get my professional qualification
You're being outrageously inconsiderate	Anger	To resolve our differences

In each case, you'd respond differently if you based your actions on your commitments rather than on your thoughts and feelings. In practice this might mean that you speak up rather than withholding your anger and feeling resentful, or listen when you'd rather be wedded to your point of view. It's not always easy to act in line with our commitments, but when we manage to do so we're usually being true to our longer-term aims and underlying values.

STEP 3:
Express and Acknowledge Feelings

As Lara found when talking to Jack and Anna about their untidy rooms, expressing your feelings is likely to have a more positive impact than venting your opinions. To communicate your feelings, you'll need to pause for a second to identify what they are; they may not come immediately to mind. When you do this, you may find that you have a bundle of feelings rather than one.

Having your feelings is very different from *becoming* your feelings. People who can't make this distinction are more likely to lash out, verbally or physically, when they feel intensely angry and frustrated. This is often the source of violent and abusive behaviour.

The other side to expressing feelings is to acknowledge them. If you're fizzing with anger on the end of a phone, a highly skilled customer service representative will start by acknowledging your feelings. They may respond with, 'I'm sorry; this must be very frustrating and disappointing for you.' Met with this response, you'll probably feel your irritation drain away, enabling you to engage in a pragmatic conversation, rather than still wanting to bark at them. On the other hand, if someone fails to listen and simply attempts to justify their position, your frustration may rise to boiling point and your words will pour out in an angry tirade.

STEP 4:
Challenge Your Truth and Logic

The ability of athletes to deal with negative emotions while under immense physical strain and mental pressure is a decisive ingredient for success. Whether it's an Olympic athlete expressing his fears before the race of his life or Lara expressing her emotions to Ethan, there's no substitute for being heard.

In the process, a transformation can take place; our thinking becomes less rigid and more malleable, meaning that we can challenge the truth and logic of what we're saying. Instead of seeing the world in black and white, we can start to see the grey. When this happens, we discover that we don't have to be dominated by our thoughts and feelings. Rather than having the awful experience that they are running amok and ruining our life, we can let them come and go and yet keep our focus on what's important to us.

> **Lesson 7: Allow your thoughts and feelings and be guided by your values**

CHAPTER
EIGHT

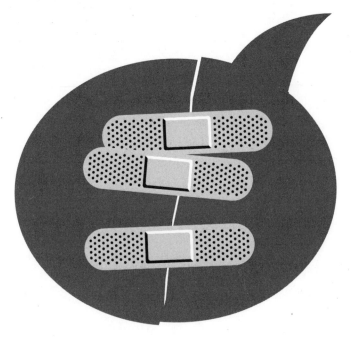

STOP FIXING PEOPLE'S PROBLEMS

Why People Don't Want Your Advice and What They Want Instead

A few summers ago, I was doing some gardening on a still, hazy afternoon when I heard a car coming down the lane. The windows must have been open, because I could hear the unmistakable sound of a child wailing, and the volume intensified as the car approached.

I don't know how long the child had been crying, but the father had clearly reached the end of his tether. When they got out of the car, their conversation went like this.

Dad: Alex, why are you crying?
Alex: I don't know!
Dad: Then STOP CRYING!!!!

This little snippet of dialogue stuck in my mind for several reasons. To start with, I could empathize with the father; he just wanted the issue to go away and there is nothing more grating than a small child who cries persistently for no obvious reason. But I could also identify with young Alex, because he may not have known *why* he felt distressed, and being told to stop crying was almost certain to make things worse. Alex was no exception and proceeded to bawl.

This brings us to the heart of the issue. More often than not, when we have an issue, it needs to be heard before it can be fixed.

THE ADDICTED ADVICE-GIVER

Even if advice is asked for – or paid for – it doesn't necessary mean that it will work. Tim Gallwey discovered this in the 1970s and transformed sports coaching in the process. He described how, as a newly qualified professional tennis coach, he would give careful and well-intended advice to eager tennis students. After a series of instructions, a student's head would be whirling with information, to the point where she could barely see the ball. Progress seemed to be slow and complicated.[15]

Gallwey became dissatisfied with his teaching methods and the progress of his students and started to focus on what he called the 'inner game' of tennis. He'd noticed that verbal instructions often decreased rather than increased the probability of someone improving their game. As a result, he broke away from traditional methods of coaching, vowing never to offer advice. Since then he's coached world champions. How can this be?

Gallwey realized that if he encouraged students to observe how they were playing their shots, without judgement, their game immediately improved. Rather than telling a student, 'You need to roll your wrist on the backhand', Gallwey's approach encouraged students to volunteer, 'I notice that I don't roll my wrist on my backhand.' Thanks to Gallwey's influence, the best sports coaches are now trained to limit the advice they give and instead ask questions that allow people to let go of self-judgements, focus on what is happening and trust their natural learning process.

When I experienced Gallwey's approach first-hand, I made more progress on my backhand in an hour than in my previous 30 years of tennis, and without a single word of advice. This was a humbling experience. It forced me to call into question my incessant desire to offer people advice, tips and solutions. I'd argue that this very common trait is probably the biggest handicap to effective practice for managers, parents, partners, teachers and ... well, all of us.

RATTLING AROUND IN THE HOUSE

Ethan, our corporate banker, has the following conversation with his mum, Lily. It doesn't go disastrously wrong, but it doesn't seem to go that well either:

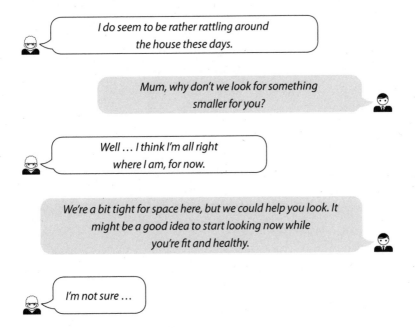

> *I do seem to be rather rattling around the house these days.*

> *Mum, why don't we look for something smaller for you?*

> *Well ... I think I'm all right where I am, for now.*

> *We're a bit tight for space here, but we could help you look. It might be a good idea to start looking now while you're fit and healthy.*

> *I'm not sure ...*

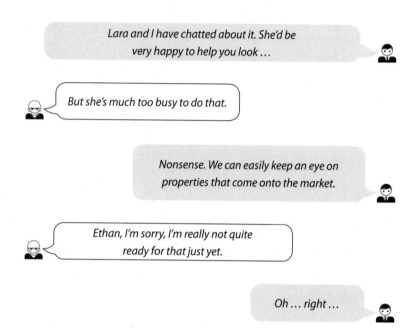

Lara and I have chatted about it. She'd be very happy to help you look …

But she's much too busy to do that.

Nonsense. We can easily keep an eye on properties that come onto the market.

Ethan, I'm sorry, I'm really not quite ready for that just yet.

Oh … right …

Later than evening, Ethan says to Lara, 'Mum complained that she was rattling around in her house and, when I suggested moving somewhere smaller, she got totally defensive. I was only trying to help.' When Lily goes home that evening, she thinks, 'That was odd. It felt like Ethan was trying to push me out of my own house.' Ethan used his mother's opening comment as a cue to solve what he identified as a problem. The real question is: what's the problem and whose problem is it? The answer's not as straightforward as you might think.

Lily *doesn't* have a problem with her house; she's merely making a throwaway comment. She's happy in her home and has lots of memories associated with it. On the other hand, Ethan does have an issue. He's concerned about what the future holds for his mother and wants her to make proactive plans while she's still healthy. Under scrutiny, it's apparent that the issue is actually his. Put another way, he's offering a solution to a problem that's worrying him and that he thinks his mother ought to be worried about too. When looked at in this way, it's clear why Lily's not very receptive to Ethan's suggestions.

If Lily does have a problem, it's that she's quite lonely and doesn't see as much of Ethan, Lara and their kids as she'd like. But Ethan takes her comment literally and now they're in the Tangle.

There are a lot of managers who tend to act in the same way as Ethan. They believe that they're not worth their salt unless they're analysing and fixing issues all day.

But there are downsides: the people they manage become worn down and disempowered by constant lecturing; besides, they're not encouraged to develop problem-solving skills themselves.

They get so addicted to fixing 'problems' that it's hard for them to change gear when they get home. Partners and children don't respond kindly to this approach and usually don't hesitate to say so.

WHAT TO DO?

STEP 1:
Give Space, Not Solutions
More often than not, someone will raise an issue because they want to be heard rather than have it fixed. They want others to understand how they're feeling and to have their personal experience acknowledged and validated. By asking a few questions and listening, without going into solution mode, Ethan would be able to identify clearly what his mother means:

> *I do seem to be rather rattling around the house these days.*

> *What do you mean, Mum?*

Well, I keep busy and active but it's obviously not been the same since I've been living on my own.
I'm fine in myself, though.

It must be quite lonely at times.

I don't want to complain. I suppose it is, but you get used to it.

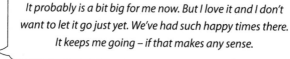

When you say you're rattling around, is that because the house is too big?

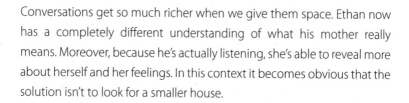

It probably is a bit big for me now. But I love it and I don't want to let it go just yet. We've had such happy times there. It keeps me going – if that makes any sense.

Conversations get so much richer when we give them space. Ethan now has a completely different understanding of what his mother really means. Moreover, because he's actually listening, she's able to reveal more about herself and her feelings. In this context it becomes obvious that the solution isn't to look for a smaller house.

STEP 2:
Give Advice When Requested

As a general rule, don't offer advice unless it's been asked for. If you work on an IT help desk, in a consumer advice bureau, or in a specialist consulting company, you're paid for your expertise. You'll need to advise people as comprehensively as you're able. But when you go home and give advice to your daughter, you need to clock whether or not she's actually asked for it. If she hasn't, at best you're likely to get a 'Yes, but...'

response to your suggestions. More likely, though, is that she'll turn off and zone out. When she sees her friends, she'll probably tell them her parents are always nagging her.

It might be difficult to accept that unsolicited advice is generally ignored so of no value, but this is indeed the case. Even so, I often find that I can't help myself. When my son went to school sports matches, I felt compelled to offer last-minute tips beforehand. It probably made me feel better for having said it but the chances are that he, or whoever's on the receiving end, ignored it.

STEP 3:
Ask What People Need – and Express Your Needs Too

People tend to be very unclear about what they need from someone in a conversation. They might say, 'I'm really having problems with Lucas at work,' without giving any indication as to whether they're just passing the time of day or whether they want you to listen, help them get clear, offer your opinion or fix the problem. In all probability they may not know themselves.

The best starting point is to ask them what they need. If they say, 'I don't think I need anything,' this is your cue to keep your wisdom to yourself – even though you might find it desperately hard to suppress. On the other hand, if they say, 'It would be good to get your advice,' this is like getting the winning numbers on a lottery ticket – inviting you to launch in with your suggestions. Like the parable of the farmer who sows his seed on fertile rather than stony ground, there's a far greater probability that your input will make a difference if it's been asked for.

There's another way of testing whether your advice might make a difference. Try offering a pearl of wisdom and listen to what you get back. If you receive objections, it's a good indication that your advice isn't wanted. Go back to listening and asking questions; find another way to support the person you're having a conversation with, though simply listening is often enough.

STEP 4:
Ask Thoughtful Questions

Asking questions is an art in itself. Voltaire got it right when he said, 'Judge a man by his questions rather than by his answers.' It requires being able to place yourself in the other person's world and consider what might help facilitate their thought process.

Great leaders and managers focus on the questions they're going to ask rather than the advice they're burning to give. This isn't to say that advice can't be given, but it's best used sparingly and with discretion.

I remember a performance appraisal I had in the early stages of my career, during which my manager asked me how I'd evaluate my year, what my aspirations were, how I thought I could build on my strengths, and what I needed from him. It was like being in a tennis lesson with Tim Gallwey. He gave a sprinkling of input, but the ratio of speaking was at least 80:20 in my favour. I came away with a renewed lightness of being. I felt heard, known and deeply supported. It still sticks in my mind 25 years later, compared to most appraisals which had little impact and quickly receded into an unmemorable blur.

> *Lesson 8: Most advice just sounds like noise*

CHAPTER
NINE

CHANGE YOUR PERSPECTIVE

How to Resolve Issues by Taking a Different Vantage Point

Look at the circles marked A and B on the next page. Which is larger? It seems obvious that the answer is B. Actually, the two circles are identical in size. To accept this fact, you may need to measure them.[16]

What we see and hear doesn't always match with reality. The problem is that we see life through our own narrow lens. Conversations can either follow a predictable path in which we trade myopic beliefs with glorious self-righteousness, or we can ask people for help to see from their vantage point, reshaping our worldview in the process. This requires a willingness to be curious.

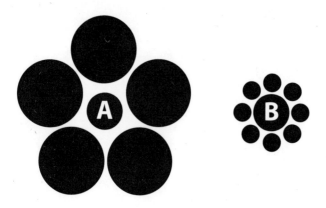

AM I BEING NARROW-MINDED?

While researching a book about a school for trainers of exotic animals, journalist and author Amy Sutherland took the concept of the alternative perspective to radical lengths.[17] Having spent years trying to turn her husband Scott into her ideal partner, she'd reached the conclusion that her strategy of nagging only made things worse. Rather than resigning herself to irritation, she decided to test the trainers' techniques on her husband.

For her particular experiment, Amy adopted the animal trainer's tried-and-tested practice of rewarding behaviour that you like and ignoring behaviour that you don't. In an article in the *New York Times*, she described how she started thanking Scott if he threw one dirty shirt into the laundry basket and kissing him if he threw in two. At the same time, she lured him away from behaviours she didn't like by coming up with attractive alternatives – when she didn't want him crowding her she'd put salsa and chips on the other side of the kitchen. And finally, she adopted the technique she'd seen the trainers use when an animal did something wrong – they didn't respond at all, following the principle that if a behaviour doesn't illicit a response, it tends to die away.

To Amy's surprise, each of these approaches worked as well on Scott as on the animals they'd been designed for. More importantly, the experiment forced her to question the view she had of her relationship.

Rather than blaming Scott for failed training attempts, she looked for new strategies. The point is that she changed her perspective and, as a result, stopped having so many blamestorming conversations.

We're all prone to sticking to die-hard routines, even when they don't work. It takes a lot less thought and effort than it does to make a difficult change. It's a bit like the man who tells his doctor that each time he has a cup of tea he gets a pain in the eye, and the doctor tells him to take the spoon out. Even when we know how to remove the source of our discomfort, it doesn't mean we'll do it. In similar fashion we fall into conversational grooves, repeating our bad habits and winding up in familiar arguments.

ADOPTING SECOND AND THIRD PERSPECTIVES

Ravi has a bad conversation about homework with Jay, his ten-year-old. Having been brought up to think that television's essentially a waste of time, and that people should be doing something more worthwhile, Ravi struggles with his children watching more than just a small amount. He gets especially grumpy about the programmes on the kids' channels, thinking they're banal and pointless.

Ravi is also tired and, in this situation, moves quickly from telling to moralizing and then threatening.

Come on, Jay, it's time to turn the TV off now and get on with your homework.

But the programme's nearly finished – it's only got 15 minutes to go.

It's a school night and you've been watching it for over an hour. You're becoming a TV junkie – you'll get square eyes.

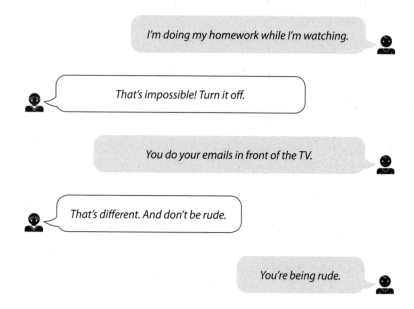

I'm doing my homework while I'm watching.

That's impossible! Turn it off.

You do your emails in front of the TV.

That's different. And don't be rude.

You're being rude.

With each comment, the volume and intensity of the conversation starts to increase. Ravi has resorted to domineering, whereas Jay is blocking. Ravi and Jay both have weapons in their armouries that they're ready to use – Ravi with the clear advantage in terms of being able to pull rank and Jay with the ability to manipulate his father emotionally.

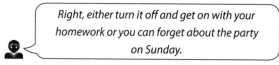

Right, either turn it off and get on with your homework or you can forget about the party on Sunday.

(Jay stands up.)

I hate you – you're mean and grumpy all the time!

(He leaves the room, slamming the door.)

Jay eventually does his homework, but he won't speak to Ravi and it spoils the atmosphere in the house. It's only at bedtime that they patch things up. To make things worse, Mia tells Ravi that he's being too hard on Jay. She and Ravi end up having an argument.

It would help if Ravi was able to take a second and third perspective. The second perspective involves Ravi putting himself in Jay's shoes for a moment. He may not get it exactly right, and he won't necessarily agree with it, but it may go something like this:

> *I'm at school all week and don't get much time to do what I want. You're on my case all the time. You don't understand what it's like for me; you keep talking about how it was for you at school but that was centuries ago. You make it sound like I don't do any work but that's unfair. You don't know what I'm doing at school anyway. At least I do my homework – you don't know how lucky you are. You think the kids' channel is rubbish but I quite enjoy it.*

Ravi could also consider a third perspective. This would be the perspective of someone watching the conversation as an independent observer who has no personal agenda to push and no vested interest in the outcome. Ravi could envisage someone whose balanced opinion he'd respect – his grandmother, for example. She always seemed to have a wise word and a level head and could be honest without making him feel that he was wrong. What would she have said? He can almost hear her voice and picture her face as she speaks:

> *Ravi, it sounds as though you feel Jay's wasting his time because watching TV is not something you value. You need to remember that he's only ten. You sound tired and he feels harshly treated by you. You'd be better off telling him how you feel and trying to figure out a solution together.*

Taking the second and third perspectives doesn't mean Ravi has to sit down with a piece of paper and write it all out. We're quite capable of considering different perspectives at the same time, just as we can safely drive a car while chatting, taking note of road signs, watching the speed limit and keeping an eye out for other vehicles.

The thing to remember is that the first, second and third perspectives are only perspectives – none of these viewpoints has a monopoly on the truth. When confronted by a disagreement our attitudes tend to become fixed, at precisely the moment when we'd benefit from being flexible. It will seem as if the first perspective is the most accurate because it's our own. But Ravi would do well to remember that he's in his living room, not a courtroom; he doesn't need to argue over 'the truth', even though his ten-year-old is making a valiant effort to do so. Neither does Ravi need to stamp his authority on the situation, which is his instinctive response when he's tired.

Having considered the second and third perspectives, Ravi can tackle the conversation in a different way and with a different tone – without making threats or moralizing. A response like the following one from Ravi won't make Jay jump for joy, but it does take his son's needs into account and is a reasonable proposal:

> *Jay, I know you need a break after a full day at school and I don't want to cut your programme off suddenly. Can we agree to turn it off in 15 minutes, at 7pm? If it hasn't finished, you can watch the end of it after you've done your homework.*

Ravi is no longer domineering the conversation and is making a conscious effort to manage his tone. Control-based strategies almost always provoke either grudging compliance or resistance. By pausing for a moment to think about your approach to a conversation, angst can be avoided without any loss of authority. Rather than seeing situations in one dimension, adopting a second and third perspective provides you with a 3D view. In the process, it allows you to see different solutions.

In the heat of a flare-up it's all too easy to forget that the most powerful and fulfilling conversations involve people sharing and examining their stories in a spirit of exchange and understanding – even if they have very different worldviews. More often than not, this leads to the creation of new and deeper levels of shared meaning.

WHAT TO DO?

STEP 1:
Get on Their Track

If my wife Sally raises something I don't want to address, I have a tendency to deflect it. I'll say, 'Let's chat about this tomorrow' or 'I'm too tired to discuss that now,' but these are blocking techniques which avoid the need for me to pause and accept that the conversation – which may not seem important or timely to me – is important to her.

Understanding someone else's perspective begins with slowing down for long enough to listen and show an interest. While doing this, it's important not to keep bringing the conversation back onto your track. Rather, keep it on their track and see what transpires.

STEP 2:
Imagine a Different Physical Position

While adopting the second perspective, make an effort to imagine yourself physically in the other person's position, looking at you. In the same way, when considering the third perspective, imagine yourself physically occupying the space between you and the other person. Doing so makes it easier to step out of your own mental world and consider a different stance.

STEP 3:

Drop the Control

It's a fact of life that we operate in hierarchies. At work, there are lines of accountability that describe who reports to whom, and even the CEO is accountable to others – whether customers, shareholders or the board of directors. In family life, there's also a degree of seniority and authority that comes with being the parent.

However, it's self-evident that managers and parents who persistently adopt strategies based on domineering, discounting or blamestorming – endlessly lecturing, moralizing or issuing threats – are largely ignored. Think about a teacher who is over-reliant on barking orders at their pupils in class. Ironically, because they command little respect, their authority is undermined. No longer able to bank on the goodwill of their students, they pull rank because it's the easiest option and because they don't have any other strings to pull. Getting the balance right is tricky, since the converse problem is not to exert any authority and to allow people to run riot around you. The moral seems to be that you can exert authority, and even hold people to account, without being belittling or overly controlling.

Generating trust clearly offers the most mileage in terms of getting the best from others, but it's hard won and easily lost. Genuinely seeking to understand another person's perspective doesn't imply that we need to take the soft option and surrender to their needs. Which of these would you rather experience: that someone more 'senior' to you took the time and trouble to adopt the second and third perspectives, then explained their decision and their reasons behind it; or that they ignored your opinion and simply told you what to do? We can put up with the latter once or twice, but it wears thin very quickly. In contrast, if someone makes genuine efforts to understand our perspective, there's a greater probability that a way forward will be found that's acceptable for both of us.

Lesson 9: Put yourself in the other person's world

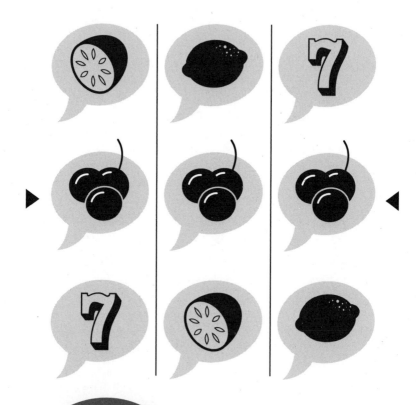

CHAPTER
TEN

DEVELOP CLEAR AGREEMENTS

Why Agreements Take the Stress out of Disagreements

During a parliamentary debate in the House of Commons, members aren't allowed to speak directly to one another. Instead, in order to abide by the rules, they have to go through the Speaker of the House. Rather than being able to tell a fellow politician that he's a loser, members have to say something like, 'Mr Speaker, as far as I'm concerned, the honourable gentleman is incompetent.' This etiquette, which might seem rather odd and certainly requires a great deal of self-control, was put in place to avoid face-to-face confrontation and all-out acrimony. During his resignation speech in 1990, Sir Geoffrey Howe managed to deliver one of the most withering critiques of a serving prime minister while referring to her throughout as 'My right honourable friend'.[18]

It's a tradition that enables members of parliament to express strong views while reducing levels of antagonism. However, they need constant reminding to stick to the third-person protocol. In one debate, an MP forgot to address the Speaker and said this about his parliamentary colleague: 'Interestingly, the government's proposal to review benefits means that if you are a woman, you should consider suffocating your husband.' The Speaker of the House immediately replied, 'It is self-evident that I am not a woman, and my wife would be extremely surprised to discover that I had a husband.'[19]

Debates are also regulated by strict codes of conduct governing what kind of language can and can't be used. When an MP crosses the line and says something considered unacceptable, it is recorded. Entries in the logbook of unparliamentary phrases differ from one country to the next. The following remark made the list after being uttered in New Zealand's parliament in 1949: 'His brains could revolve inside a peanut shell for a thousand years without touching the sides.'[20] It's the kind of humour that might get children interested in politics, but it's blacklisted in parliamentary debate – at least, in New Zealand.

PREDICTING RELATIONSHIP BREAKDOWNS

While they're in the House, MPs have to stick to established ground rules, but the shackles are off when it comes to people's language at home. There are no formal rules stopping us from accusing each other of being liars, cheats and losers, but there are consequences. Dan and Beth have free rein to say what they like to each other in the heat of the moment, but they'll have to accept that what they say may impact on their relationship, particularly if it becomes hurtful.

Dr John Gottman and Dr Bob Levenson are world-leading experts on relationship analysis and the characteristics of marital stability. During a study in 1983, they set up a Love Lab to study the way that couples conducted difficult conversations. They discovered that in 96 per cent of cases, the way people handled the first three minutes of a conflict discussion determined how it would go for its duration. If they began the conversation in a critical manner – triggering each of the warning lights outlined in this book – it seemed to set the tone for their relationship. What's more, with over 90 per cent accuracy Gottman and Levenson found that they could predict the longer-term success or failure of any relationship, based purely on observing the way a couple discussed an area of conflict.[21]

Gottman and Levenson were so surprised by the initial results of their research that they thought it might be down to chance. However, time and again, their findings were reaffirmed. In situations where a relationship had broken down, they discovered that the way partners had been conducting their conversations hadn't grown or evolved while they'd been together. The relationships that failed tended to be those in which the couples they observed were interacting almost identically to the way in which they'd been interacting when they'd first been studied, four years earlier. Gottman and Levenson's research confirms, beyond all doubt, that the way we conduct our conversations determines the success of our relationships.

DIFFERENT AGREEMENTS FOR DIFFERENT CONVERSATIONS

It's easy to make a false assumption and think that having clear agreements can stifle conversation. On the contrary, agreements can allow conversations to flow, preventing them from becoming tangled up. I've worked with hundreds of teams all over the world and the best ones have clear rules of engagement. These aren't imposed from on-high but are made and owned by each team member.

Having agreements enables people to know where they stand and how to tackle problems or disagreements as they arise.

When banker Ethan is asked what he does for a living he often says, 'I'm a professional meeting attender.' People laugh but they know what he means. Many of us spend too much time in meetings that are poorly conducted and give a negative return for all our time and effort.

A typical day for Ethan might go like this:

08.30–09.30

Team meeting to start the day. The quality of the conversation is poor and some team members are checking emails or sending text messages.

> *What agreement is needed? Barring an emergency, agree not to use phones during meetings.*

11.00–12.00

Ethan has a meeting to discuss the marketing plan. The conversation sprawls until people get frustrated. 'We seem to have gone way off the point,' someone moans after 45 minutes.

> *What agreement is needed? Begin each meeting with a clear intention, and decide what's in scope and what's out of scope for your conversation, so the parameters are clear.*

12.30–13.30

Ethan gets back to his desk and find 40 new emails in his inbox. He skims through them all, but only a few are directly relevant to him.

> *What agreement is needed? Establish email protocols so that people don't waste time reading unnecessary messages.*

15.00–17.00

Ethan's boss sets up a meeting to develop a new proposal. It's meant to be a creative discussion but people are quick to trample on each other's ideas.

> *What agreement is needed? When exploring new opportunities, make time to listen to each other's ideas, even if some of them seem outlandish. At a later stage you'll need to challenge those same ideas and test if they're viable, but don't shoot them down too early.*

20.15

While putting the kids to bed, Ethan takes a call from work about an IT issue. Lara starts complaining, saying he's always working. When Ethan tells her it's an emergency, she asks him why there seems to be a new one every evening. It's a bad end to the day.

> *What agreement is needed? Discuss ways of dealing with issues around working at home and protecting family time. As the boundaries between home and work become increasingly blurred, we need more robust mechanisms for switching off.*

Agreements that are appropriate to the context of a relationship, team or project need to be developed and agreed. Once established, they'll allow you to navigate your way through difficult conversational territory.

In the lead-up to the 2012 Olympic Games in London, I worked with the teams building the stadiums and athletes' village. For the first time since the introduction of the modern Olympics in 1896, nobody was killed during the construction process, in spite of the fact that 46,000 people delivered 77 million hours of work.[22] Far from being down to luck, this was the product of people raising their individual concerns about safety at every level of the project. Everyone understood that, by working on the Olympics, they were entering a psychological contract in which they had permission to tackle difficult conversations with each other and could do so without fear of negative consequences.

Many people dread the prospect of conducting conversations within large groups, often for fear that the situation will devolve into anarchy. Establishing ground rules at a meeting's outset is essential to avoid this. For example, I'll always ask people to raise challenges and questions – albeit in a respectful way – in the meeting rather than out of earshot at the coffee machine, so that we have an opportunity to resolve them. When jointly created, ground rules provide the foundation for meaningful conversations.

HAVING AGREEMENTS AT HOME

The idea of having an agreement might sound a bit official, or even rather corporate. Despite this, agreements are even more important at home. Karam and Kartari Chand were married for more than 90 years – reportedly longer than any couple in UK – before Karam recently died at the age of 110. Karam said he loved Kartari so much that he wanted to spend another 90 years by her side.[23] The question everyone asked is how they managed to keep their relationship intact for so many years. One of the secrets of their success was the way they gave time to one another.

'Listen to each other,' Karam explained. 'The most important thing in a relationship is to listen. People don't listen any more because they are too busy with work and TV. Listen to your loved ones' problems and concerns every day.' We all know the wisdom of Karam's advice, but it's not an easy commitment to stick to. Opportunities to listen might feel as if they need to be jammed into our hectic schedules. General exhaustion, work overspill, devices, social media and family commitments can leave us feeling that we don't have time for proper conversation.

The Marriage Course, developed by Nicky and Sila Lee, makes a very clear recommendation. Once a week, couples should spend at least two hours together in uninterrupted time, sharing their hopes, anxieties, excitements, worries and achievements as a means of building intimacy. Ideas such as this seem blindingly obvious, yet personal experience suggests they can be absurdly difficult to practise. Life gets in the way, but our relationships are at the heart of our lives. Managing this contradiction gets even more difficult if we haven't established clear agreements with each other.

WHAT TO DO?

STEP 1:

Turn Expectations into Agreements

Ethan's productivity and sense of fulfilment at work could be radically improved if he established some simple but explicit agreements with his colleagues. Whatever the context, focus on the few that will make the biggest difference rather than developing a long list; for example, having a genuine commitment to listen to each other during work meetings will transform the effectiveness of your time together.

Conversations can fragment without an argument having to break out. Sheer earnestness to be heard or to get a point across often leads to an absence of listening. Whether it's because we grew up in a large family, sat in a class at school with 30 other children or have highly vocal work colleagues, we learn that the world is not going to wait for us to collect our thoughts. There seems to be an unspoken understanding that we need to muscle our way into conversations to ensure our voice gets heard. When you're sitting in work meetings, you know that the pauses between people speaking will be short, and that you'll have to jump in quickly to get into that ever-so-tiny gap. It doesn't have to be so, and having clear agreements helps mitigate this impulse.

For several decades I've worked with organizational leadership teams, and I'm often struck by the inefficiency of their interactions. All it takes is for one person to offer an opinion, at which point the meeting becomes a free-for-all. In one company, we sought to negate this tendency by creating strict meeting agreements. As each member of the team reported back on their functional area, they had to signpost whether their input was for information, discussion or a decision. If it was for information, there would be no debate. If it was for discussion, an exchange of views was warmly welcomed. And if it was for a decision, they had to clarify – like the umpire in a tennis match – who would make the relevant line-calls. Extrapolated across the year, this small change led to clearer thinking, better decision-making and more effective action.

STEP 2:
Remind Each Other of Your Agreements

Holding each other to your agreements isn't always easy. Dan and Beth have agreed that they won't let the sun go down on an argument. They'll need to remind each other of this when they're in the Bad Place and want to be left alone to sulk. If Beth does so by blamestorming, she might say:

> *Now I suppose you're going to sulk all evening, instead of talking things through.*

This approach won't help. It would be better if she let her emotions settle after an argument and then tried:

> *We said we'd never go to sleep on an argument. Can we talk things through, so we can get them resolved?*

If they manage to sit down together, having clear ground rules will really help their conversation. Perhaps most importantly, they need to agree that they'll listen to each other without interruption. Rather than making mental notes of barbed one-liners in response to what they're hearing, they need to listen from the second and third perspectives. Doing this will help loosen their attachment to their own version of the truth. It doesn't mean that Beth needs to share Dan's opinion on the situation, or vice versa. But by accepting the validity of each other's perspective, they're more likely to release themselves from a position of righteousness and create a joint way forward.

Holding each other to your values, in the easy times and the tough times, is the basis for strong relationships and strong communities. As the saying goes, 'Good fences make good neighbours.'

Lesson 10: Agreements can set you free

CHAPTER
ELEVEN

SET THE CONTEXT

How to Prevent Misunderstanding and Defensive Responses

Sailing the high seas in the 16th century in search of new lands must have felt like heading into a vast chasm of uncertainty. Unpredictable weather, enemy fleets, opportunistic pirates, sketchy maps and rudimentary navigational equipment would have made it impossible to predict a safe return. When the scurvy-suffering, bleary-eyed lookout finally shouted, 'Land ahoy!,' the crew members must have had feelings of disquiet. They didn't know if they'd spend the evening dancing around a casserole pot with their new friends, or were destined to be the meal in the pot.

Such a precarious state of affairs led ships to the practice of raising flags to state their nationality and intentions as they advanced toward a territory, indicating whether they were friend or foe. This system has endured through the centuries and has been written into the United

Nations Convention on the Law of the Sea. Flags state where you're coming from and heading to and, you hope, herald your arrival to a welcoming reception committee.

Though not quite so perilous, conversations can sometimes feel like being on the high seas because:

- they don't tend to follow a straight line.
- people don't always manage to say what they mean.
- others can't be relied on to react as we'd like, or may not agree with our point of view.
- people may keep their intentions under wraps.
- the interaction moves at a helter-skelter pace and we don't have the luxury of long pauses to assess what someone's said before we reply.

In the face of this, it's vital that we operate our own flag system to let people know where we're coming from and heading to. If we fail to do so, we shouldn't be surprised if they react defensively, as a way of coping with the unexpected demands of a conversation – especially when it's particularly difficult.

The words themselves represent the content of a conversation; the context is what surrounds them. It includes the preceding and subsequent words, the tone they're spoken in, body language and the intention behind the words. Being able to grasp both content and context simultaneously enables us to apprehend meaning and navigate a conversation's direction.

SEEING PART OF THE PICTURE

If the context isn't clear, it's easy for a conversation to fall into mixed messages. We're adept at recognizing when someone means balmy rather than barmy, cereal rather than serial or elicit rather than illicit, because of the context in which the word is used. Understanding a person's intentions is more tricky. I recently sent a perfectly polite email to a client with a series of questions that were relevant to the project I was working on. He replied with a one-liner stating:

```
This feels like ground-hog day.
```

He then proceeded to answer each question in the body of my email with comments that ended with exclamation marks such as, 'I confirmed this yesterday!'

Most people would describe me as even-tempered but, after receiving several emails like this, I was irritated by his behaviour and offered to stop the work altogether. It was only a week or two later that I realized that the man was under the most unbearable stress and felt at breaking point. He was sinking under the relentless demands of work and was a sleep-deprived parent of young children, and his mental health was taking a battering. The point is that I didn't appreciate the wider context, and he could have done a better job of explaining his context by sending a one-liner like this:

```
Sorry, immensely stressful times here. Please see brief
responses below.
```

Conversations go wrong when the context isn't understood by both parties, or is misconstrued. You may think you're having a playful conversation but your partner takes offence, or you're trying to be helpful but come across as interfering and dominating. While it's easier to lay the blame on someone else for getting the wrong end of the stick, we can usually do more to make our context clear.

My wife Sally has a talent for accents and can slip seamlessly into different dialects. If she's annoyed that I haven't washed up my dishes (again), she might adopt a Cornish, Irish or Australian accent. It allows her to signal her frustration while being lighthearted and reducing the likelihood of an argument.

THE ROLE OF CONTEXT

In modern English the use of the word 'context' can be traced to the early 15th century, though its etymology reaches back to the Latin word *contextus*. The ancient use of the word meant 'to join together by weaving.' By implication, this involves bringing different parts together to create a whole.

With information flying at us through our devices in byte-sized pieces, the world can feel increasingly fragmented. It's estimated that each day we're exposed to a thousand advertisements from the TV, internet, billboards, radio and newspapers. Over the course of a week, the information we absorb could fill a computer's hard drive. We're overloaded with content, but it doesn't necessarily come with an accompanying context, and it's our job to make sense of it all.

People are more motivated at work when they understand the context in which they're doing it: why it's important, what value it brings and the difference it will make if they strive to perform well. If they feel like they're insignificant cogs in a corporate machine, they'll invest minimal effort and care. Gallup's Meta-Analysis study (2020) shows that companies in the highest quartile in terms of employee engagement have 81 per cent less absenteeism and a 66 per cent increase in staff wellbeing, not to mention vastly superior turnover and profitability.[24]

In these organizations, leaders invest more time ensuring people feel included, involved and connected to a higher purpose. I worked with one company that ranked 'outstanding' every year in the *Sunday Times* 'Best Place to Work' index. The CEO dedicated a month every year to roadshows with his teams across Europe. He used this time to communicate the strategy but, more importantly, to listen. It's hardly surprising that 84 per cent of his staff said they had great faith in him as their CEO, which was one of the highest scores for any UK company.

Those who go the extra mile in service of a cause, project or organization do so because of the context. They see opportunities for themselves and a meaningful vision for the future, and they feel that they're being fully supported in, and acknowledged for, their work.

WHERE IT GOES WRONG

In the following examples the context isn't clearly communicated, leading to unintended consequences:

1. Mia, who's a social worker, is given some feedback by her manager. She's highly regarded at work and is seen as someone with the potential for promotion in the coming year, but her boss assumes she knows this and starts their conversation by saying:

> *As you know, we've gathered some feedback from your colleagues and there are a few areas that have come to light that I want to discuss.*

Mia's left feeling offended as well as unsure about where she stands in relation to her long-term future as a social worker, while her boss is surprised at her reaction to his comments and by her defensive demeanour.

2. Ravi's been assigned to a challenging technology project for the last few months. While he's working on it late one evening, he gets an email that's been written by the IT director, forwarded to him by a colleague:

```
Sorry. Got some issues related to the new release.
Will need to pause the project. Hopefully back on
track very soon.
```

This email comes out of the blue and Ravi only understands a fragment of the background to the decision. Without the wider context he ends up feeling totally disenfranchised. Another company has recently approached him with a job offer and he decides to talk to them.

3. Diane is headteacher at the local primary school, and Beth's boss. She has a 15-year-old son called Ben and worries that he's destined for academic failure. In turn, Ben feels nagged by her. Every time the subject is mentioned, their conversation escalates, which only makes the situation worse.

4. Rather than writing separate replies to work emails, Diane tends to write comments alongside the messages she's received. In order for her notes to stand out, she writes short answers in RED CAPITALS such as: YES, NO, NOT SURE – NEED TO TALK. Yui, who's Japanese, is a member of Diane's teaching staff. She finds Diane's replies rude and feels that her boss is domineering. For Diane it's simply a time-saving device.

In each case, problems arise not so much due to the content, but because the conversation's context hasn't been established to enable both parties to share a mutual understanding.

WHAT TO DO?

STEP 1:
Put Up Your Flag

The conversation between Mia and her boss would have progressed more positively if he'd given some thought to how he might have set it up – perhaps beginning like this:

> *Mia, you're highly valued and we're really keen for you to progress to a more senior role. You're already exceptionally strong in some areas and will need to develop in others.*

Mia's boss may want to find out more about her ambitions and ask her to self-evaluate areas for potential improvement, as well as giving her his own feedback. He can still communicate this in a straightforward and direct manner – there's no need to prevaricate – but first, he should set a context in which Mia can hear what he has to say with openness and positivity.

STEP 2:

Acknowledge Concerns

You'll establish a stronger connection with someone you're talking to if you can reflect what they may be thinking or feeling.

It would make a difference to Ravi if his boss Steve said:

> *Ravi, I know you've worked flat-out for the last three months to get this project over the line, and I know it's frustrating and demoralizing when these things get pulled at the last minute. But I really am extremely grateful for your efforts. This is the background to the decision – just so you understand what's going on …*

STEP 3:

Express Commitment

Having drawn the conclusion that Diane's nagging him all the time, it becomes difficult for teenager Ben to listen with the feeling that she can really help him. Diane needs to engage Ben by making her commitment clear and bringing her subtext into the open:

> *I know I sound like a constant nag. I'm not out to spoil your fun, and I'm not expecting A grades in everything either. But I do want you to have choices about what you do after leaving school. I want to be able to support you but I'm struggling to know how. Can we talk?*

STEP 4:
Seek to Understand Each Other's Context

Yui doesn't say anything to Diane about her emails, but when she's at home she complains to her boyfriend about Diane's lack of courtesy. It has a strong effect on her motivation at work.

Meanwhile, Diane is oblivious to the cultural nuances causing offence for Yui. If she was aware of the issue, she could modify her emails – or set the context by explaining why she replies as she does. What Yui doesn't realize is that Diane's terse email responses are a means of coping with a hundred messages a day, many of which she has to catch up on late at night. Their failure to understand each other's context leads to the Tangle.

Diane and Yui's example highlights our need to talk to one another about our individual style of communication. In any aspect of life, misunderstandings are inevitable. What's important, though, is to check regularly what we need to be doing more or less of – or what we should be continuing to do – in our interactions with those around us. As a consequence, the job of navigating our way through difficult conversations is made so much easier.

> *Lesson 11: Content always sits inside context*

CHAPTER
TWELVE

CLEAR UP
THE MESS

How to Say 'Sorry' and Clear up Disagreements

There are few words more weighted with meaning than 'sorry'. According to one survey, in the UK alone it's uttered 368 million times every day.[25] It's a word that's developed multiple meanings ranging from complete acceptance of responsibility to an exclamation we make when someone bumps into us, which roughly translates as: 'Look where you're going!'

The history of literature proves that we've always been confused about what 'sorry' actually means. Plato's *Apology* is his account of a speech made by Socrates in 399 BC that doesn't contain a sniff of an apology. Put on trial for not recognizing the gods, Socrates sets the scene by saying that his accusers 'have hardly spoken a word of truth'. What follows is a withering verbal attack. Plato's title only makes sense when it's explained that ἀπολογία (or *apologia*) means 'defence' in Greek.[26]

Fast-forward to 1606 and Shakespeare's Macbeth appears on stage after murdering King Duncan, with bloody dagger in hand. Macbeth has cleared his way to the crown, but instead of experiencing delight he states grimly, 'This is a sorry sight'.[27] In contrast to Socrates' confident defence, Macbeth's 'sorry' is laden with remorse, guilt, paranoia and the onset of madness.

Carry on to the present day and we see that a simple word can still convey multiple meanings:

- I'm sorry and I take full responsibility.
- I'm sorry but, for the record, I was right.
- I'm sorry, but you had it coming.
- I'm sorry, but I was an innocent victim of circumstances.
- I'm sorry, but you did over-react.
- I'm sorry, but I can't remember a thing and therefore can't be responsible.
- I'm sorry, but you provoked me and therefore it's technically your fault.
- I'm sorry if I'm wrong, but I doubt it.
- I'm sorry. Now where's your apology?
- I'm sorry you misread what I meant.
- I've said sorry, so why can't you move on?
- On the advice of my PR agent, I'm sorry.

With the exception of the first, each of these is likely to spark another row, conforming to Oscar Wilde's advice: 'Always forgive your enemies – nothing annoys them so much.'

A genuine 'sorry'– in the sense of taking responsibility without justification – is extremely powerful because there's no inference of blame or defence, and no hidden agenda. It's simply 'sorry'. If I apologize to you, it doesn't guarantee that you will accept it, or that any hurt caused is resolved, but it's a clear acknowledgement of my role in something that didn't work for you.

THE MESSY NATURE OF CONVERSATION

Clearing up the mess doesn't always have to involve offering an apology, but it does demand thinking about what will settle, heal or even enhance a situation or relationship. Without making any excuses for poor conduct, we have to accept that conversation can be a chaotic business and doesn't unfold in straight lines. It can be bewildering, fast moving, turbulent, exhilarating and infuriating in equal measure. As such, it would be ridiculous to imagine that you're going to get all your conversations right.

It's worth noting that people have different ways of dealing with conflict. Some people report high levels of fulfilment in their personal relationship while rarely tackling disagreements head-on. They've developed ways of simply 'getting over it' when they clash with their partner, without having to delve into the details once they've both cooled down. There's a sound principle behind this. Making space and creating distance allows time to take the second and third perspectives, enabling both parties to get down from their high horse and move on without a residue of ill feeling.

However, it's unrealistic to expect that we can go through life without having a difficult conversation from time to time. Whether we've been in the Tangle, the Big Argument, the Bad Place or the Lockdown, there are occasions when we need to revisit a situation, if only to untangle crossed wires, repair emotional damage or work out how to avoid a situation in which the same pattern of disagreement repeats itself.

How can we increase the odds of a constructive outcome?

THE LOCKDOWN

It's worth focusing on the Lockdown, as this can be the toughest situation to address. Imagine someone metaphorically pulling down the portcullis on any further communication and putting up a large 'No Entry' sign. The person is hurt or angry, or both, and doesn't want to talk. Sometimes there can be a case for allowing time and space for a natural healing process to take place, rather than trying to force the issue and creating even more acrimony. Equally, having the tools to address this kind of situation would give you choice and the potential to resolve things more rapidly.

Headteacher Diane has a flare-up with her 17-year-old daughter Abby, who demonstrates zero tact when she suddenly comes out with, 'Can you pick me up at 11pm from the party on Thursday?' Abby's timing is impeccably bad: Diane's had a shocking day at work and has just pulled a burned pizza out of the oven. To make matters worse, she has no recollection of a party on Thursday and the idea of an 11pm pick-up on a school evening is inconceivable when Abby is meant to be revising for her exams. She's riled by her daughter's expectant tone and doesn't help matters by twice referring to Abby as 'young lady', in a way that emphasizes her own rank and discounts Abby's. The conversation concludes with slammed doors, Abby in the Lockdown in her bedroom and an untouched meal going cold on the kitchen table.

In retrospect, Diane could have avoided an argument if she'd deferred it. Getting the timing right is vital. She could have put off confronting Abby until a better moment, giving herself more thinking time in the process:

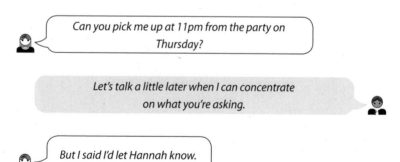

> Can you pick me up at 11pm from the party on Thursday?

> Let's talk a little later when I can concentrate on what you're asking.

> But I said I'd let Hannah know.

Well, I'm sorry. Hannah will have to wait.

 Can I just tell her 'yes'?

Please, Abby, let's talk a bit later. I'm tired and rather busy right now. You'll get a much better response if you give me an hour.

However, now that the damage is done, Diane is aware that the impasse with Abby could rumble on for a few days. She decides to tackle the situation immediately rather than letting it fester. This isn't easy, since the golden rule when tackling the Lockdown is to allow time for an abundance of listening and Diane doesn't actually feel as if she's done anything wrong. The following exchange is likely to make matters worse:

(Diane peers around the bedroom door.)

Abby, I'm sorry I barked at you.

(Abby stares at her phone.)

Abby, please ... can we talk?

 I don't want to discuss it. I can't believe you said no ...

> *Abby, come on. It's hardly fair to put all the blame on me!*

With her last comment Diane has allowed herself to be drawn into blamestorming, and the row will ignite again. This time it could get even worse. It's vital that Diane can park her side of the story for a while, and listen.

GETTING BACK IN COMMUNICATION

To get the conversation going, Diane needs to recognize Abby's feelings and ask open questions without rising to Abby's barbed comments. She also needs to consider Abby's viewpoint by adopting the second perspective:

> *I know you feel very upset and aggrieved about this. Can you tell me what the plan was for Thursday?*

 > *I told you about two weeks ago. You never remember anything. Hannah's having a birthday party …*

> *OK. I don't remember. Can you tell me again?*

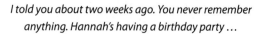 > *You do remember! I said we were having drinks at hers and a meal out. There's eight of us and Thursday's the only day Hannah can make before the end of term.*

> OK. Let me just check what you're saying …

If Diane can stick with the conversation and ask questions without making Abby feel wrong, there'll be a point where there's enough space for her to express her own feelings. When she does, she'll be better off naming the issues that were in the subtext of their flare-up earlier. These have more to do with underlying feelings than with the timing of the party itself.

> *I'm worried that you've got exams soon and that you'll run out of revision time. I'm also quite stressed and tired and really don't relish the idea of coming out at 11 o'clock to pick you up. We did make a deal that you wouldn't go out in the week during term time, but I don't want to spoil your fun and I know you need a break now and again.*

If Diane can express her subtext without dropping into blamestorming, it would open the door for Abby to express her subtext too:

> *Mum, if you come any earlier, I'll be totally humiliated. Everyone will say I was tucked up in bed while they were still out. I know you've got a lot on at the moment, but I promise I won't be late. I can see if Hannah's mum will drop me home.*

As their affinity gets restored, they quite naturally move into negotiation and, with a new-found willingness to compromise, reach a mutually acceptable solution. To get it to this point, Diane has had to bite her lip and let Abby have her say, at least during the conversation's early stages. By keeping her equanimity and detaching from her instinct to react, Diane has created the space for communication. The heaviness of the conversation begins to lift and some humour – though ironic at first – creeps back in.

This doesn't mean that Diane becomes a doormat – she doesn't *have* to acquiesce to Abby's request – but it's vital she listens either way. She also needs to explain the context of her response; without doing so, they will get dragged into a brawl and Diane is likely to pull rank. In the end they do reach a solution, with clear ground rules around Abby's attitude and timing. This needs to come toward the end of the interaction. If Diane starts to lay down the law too early, things will deteriorate.

WHAT TO DO?

The principles of listening and taking an alternative perspective are relevant both when seeking to prevent a conversation from going wrong and when trying to get out of a messy conversational situation. There are several practices to keep in mind.

STEP 1:

Apologize Without Justification

It's probably better not to apologize at all if you're going to follow it up by attempting to justify yourself or blame someone else. Apology and blame are like oil and water. If you're going to say sorry, do it without any sense of self-righteousness or inference that you deserve a sainthood for doing so. There's nothing that will rile other people more.

STEP 2:

Ask Open Questions and Hear Them out

If someone's in the Lockdown you need to ask open questions that invite them to express their feelings and point of view. Again, don't venture into this territory unless you're willing to listen to what they have to say, even if you think it's untrue or unjustified. Your job is to hear them out fully, letting them know you're listening by reflecting what they said back to them – challenging though this might be:

So you're saying you think it's unfair of me to expect you to …

I make no promises that it's an easy process, but demonstrating that you can listen, and hear what's being said without interrupting, can help someone move out of the Lockdown.

STEP 3:
Put Your Own Story on Hold
If you're going to truly listen to someone else's perspective, you need to put your story on hold until you've heard theirs. While you do this, your job isn't to prepare your own defence – unless, of course, you're in a court of law, in which case the rules are entirely different and a judge will determine the outcome.

When you do get an opportunity to speak, it's worth acknowledging that you're recounting your story as opposed to the truth of the matter – even though you may feel that the two are the same thing. If you can accept that the other person has a legitimate version of events, you can listen to understand it rather than constructing evidence in your mind about why they are wrong.

STEP 4:
Get Back to What's Important
Whenever I work with people who are locked in a disagreement, I'm amazed at how often the chasm between those involved doesn't look nearly as wide – or can even disappear altogether – once they're in open communication with each other. They often see that they have the same commitments and values even though they have different styles of expression or views about how to deliver on these commitments. Once they've listened to one another, they naturally start to look for ways forward. However, the process has to start with listening.

While conflict can be healthy, it's important to remember that there are two types – one is proactive and productive, the other is bitter and toxic.

To keep a conversation healthy, you need to navigate your way through differences of opinion without running into treacherous currents, and have tools to repair the damage if the conversation goes awry. As long as you've genuinely accepted your part in the problem, saying 'sorry' is a good start.

Lesson 12: Say 'sorry' without giving your story

CHAPTER
THIRTEEN

ADAPT YOUR LANGUAGE

How to Flex Your Style for Different People

Chimps and bonobos are our closest genetic cousins, and we share around 99 per cent of our DNA with them. Frans de Waal began studying primates in the 1970s, at a time when the prevailing research was focused on their negative traits of competitiveness and aggression. To his surprise, he uncovered a compelling body of evidence that primates can surrender their personal needs for the benefit of the group, demonstrate reciprocity and even show empathy.

De Waal observed chimps reconciling after a conflict through embracing and hugging, and found that a chimp who's received an extra-long groom is more likely to reciprocate by sharing her next meal with her groomer. Perhaps most extraordinary are his studies relating to fairness. De Waal discovered that, if chimps were rewarded with a highly prized grape for performing a task, but saw other chimps being given a less coveted piece of cucumber for the same task, they would refuse to eat the grape – an act of solidarity equivalent to a trade union protest.

I particularly love the story that de Waal tells in *Mama's Last Hug* about a chimp called Atlanta who held her hand between her own legs – even though she wasn't pregnant – while her best friend called May was giving birth. In doing so, she mimicked and identified with the mother's situation.[28] While mimicking isn't proof of empathy, research has clearly shown that both humans and other species in the animal kingdom have the ability to feel what others are feeling.

MAINTAINING AFFILIATION

While chimps and bonobos demonstrate remarkable social aptitude, humans take this obsession to a whole different level. Armed with our large pre-frontal cortex and mastery of language, we are physiologically optimized for the tricky job of navigating our relational landscape. A key weapon in our armoury is the ability to surmise what's happening in another person's head – their beliefs, feelings and thoughts – which is known as theory of mind. To assist us in this challenge, we're the only animal with a clearly visible white sclera – otherwise known as the whites of the eyes – which makes it easier for us to identify where people are looking and what they are thinking.

Being highly sophisticated communication machines doesn't mean that we are without flaws. One of our shortcomings is that we find it surprisingly difficult to adapt our communication style for different people and situations. Each of us has our preferred ways of thinking and speaking, which become entrenched patterns. Some of us are more action-oriented, while others are more relationship-oriented. Some are naturally extroverted while others are reflective. Some gravitate towards structure and detail, while others are captivated by ideas and possibilities. Wherever our preferences collide, frustration and irritation are likely to ensue, to the point that relationships can break down.

SPEAKING THEIR LANGUAGE

Ethan is a great example of someone who makes logical decisions and doesn't welcome surprises. He needs time to consider a suggestion, weigh up the options, gather evidence and then come to a conclusion. In contrast, this isn't Lara's style at all. She wants the freedom to explore and discuss ideas without constraint.

Their differing styles provoke an argument when Lara raises the idea of a home improvement project. She feels it would be a perfect solution for their growing family, but she makes the mistake of using her personal style when introducing the idea, which pushes Ethan into blocking and discounting.

> *When we get the kitchen done, I'd like to get an architect to draw up plans for adding an extension on top – to use for another bathroom.*

> *Woah ... hang on a minute. Where did that come from?*

> *There's no need to 'Woah' about it. It'll add stacks of value to the house and it'll be really useful when we've got guests.*

> *Sure, and it will cost a fortune. Besides, we'll never recover the money. I don't see the point in paying an architect to draw up plans for something we're not going to do.*

When Lara says, 'I want to get an architect', Ethan hears, 'I've decided to get an architect'. This gets them off to a bad start. He reacts to the fact that she doesn't seem to be taking a methodical approach. Meanwhile, his response makes Lara feel that he's being dismissive and defensive. 'After all,' she says to herself, 'it's only an idea and he hasn't given it any consideration.' But Ethan's been caught unprepared. He doesn't see the point in encouraging an idea that he hasn't thought through. The conversation moves into blamestorming:

> *The problem is – whenever I have an idea, you manage to squash it with your big 'finance director' shoes.*

> *That's not true. It would help if you thought your ideas through first.*

> *What? Have I got the intelligence of an amoeba?*

> *It's got nothing to do with intelligence. If you're going to employ an architect, you …*

> *Yeah, yeah … you need to think it through. In case you forgot, I'm not one of your minions at work …*

Lara is triggered by Ethan's tone. She feels as though he's discounting her capability, which leaves her feeling diminished and undervalued in their relationship. It would have helped if Lara had initiated the conversation in a different way. Here's how she might have started:

> *Do you think we could have a chat about an idea I've had for the house sometime?*

> *Oh, what's that?*

> *It doesn't have to be now, but sometime would be good.*

> *No, now's fine.*

Having gained Ethan's attention, Lara may want to set the context so that he knows how to listen. This will avoid the conversation going off the rails.

> *Please remember this is only an idea.*
> *I'm not about to make a sudden decision or*
> *rush into anything.*

> *OK, let's hear it.*

Lara's thought about how to broach the subject in Ethan's style. She takes a methodical approach:

> *You know what a pain it is when we have*
> *anyone to stay, with only the one toilet and*
> *bathroom upstairs?*

> *Yeah …*

> *I noticed Number 7's on the market again. They put in a kitchen,*
> *like we're going to do, but they also built an extension upstairs for*
> *an extra bedroom. The house has gone on the market for*
> *£150,000 more than they paid for it. It got me thinking, since the*
> *layout of the house is identical to ours.*

> *Oh … so your plan is to do the same thing?*

 > *Well, the builders have got to make a flat roof for the new kitchen and since they're here anyway … I just thought it might be worth exploring.*

This is a much better start. Lara's introduced her idea in a logical and systematic way. She knows Ethan's going to need to mull it over, so she doesn't push him. She's taking it one step at a time.

EXPECT CONCERNS AND LISTEN TO THEM

When a new idea is introduced, Ethan's concerns will always rise to the surface – it's simply his method of mental processing. If Lara can go at Ethan's pace, she will get a more positive response:

> *It's all very well to say it's selling for £150,000 more, but how much of that is down to the extension? House prices have gone up anyway.*

 > *Quite.*

> *I guess I could do some research.*

 > *That's what I was thinking.*

> *If we were ever going to do it, it would be when the builders are in. And it's true, the cost of moving is astronomical.*

 > *Absolutely.*

> *OK, there's lots to consider. I'm not sure if it's a good idea, but I'll sleep on it.*

Lara's done the perfect job. The best thing she could do was seed the idea. She's got Ethan thinking and she notices him researching data on house prices the following day. It feels as though they're working in partnership, rather than in opposition.

Just as Lara has adapted her communication style to fit Ethan's, he could benefit from being more open-minded in response to her ideas rather than being quick to grill her underlying logic. This would allow her to feel more equal and valued in their relationship. He could do this by saying, 'Tell me more', rather than raising questions and concerns, and then listening more attentively to what she has to say. After all, her initial feelings may be right. Ethan and Lara's processing styles are not gender-exclusive; they reflect Ethan's preference for logic-based decisions and Lara's preference for feeling-based ones. I've seen this dynamic reversed in numerous couples. Once you've grasped the way a partner, colleague or child processes information, you can adapt the way you communicate with them. The corresponding impact on your sense of connection and your ability to have difficult conversations cannot be overstated.

WHAT TO DO?

STEP 1:

Pay Attention to the Clues

Remember that language doesn't lie. Like vapour trails from a plane, people's language is always leaving clues behind them, telling you what's important for them.

For example, when Ethan says, 'There's lots to consider' and 'I'll sleep on it,' he is signalling to Lara that he values having time to reflect on the idea of the house extension and doesn't want to feel pushed into a decision. Equally, when Lara says, 'Please remember this is only an idea,' she is telling Ethan that she likes to explore possibilities without having the constraint of producing a project plan and a budget. To the extent that they can each pick up these signals, they can adapt their communication style. Without doing so, the same frustrations will repeat over and over in their relationship.

STEP 2:

Create Rapport

Numerous studies have shown the effectiveness of mirroring people's language, pace of speech, volume and body language. Doing so deepens our sense of rapport and affinity with each other.

If one person is speaking at a hundred miles an hour and the other talks in a more considered fashion, frustration will ensue. The talkative person may feel like she's trying to get blood out of a stone, while the more reserved person feels washed overboard by the torrent of words. Alternatively, a person who tends to dispense with the niceties and get straight to the point may struggle when speaking to an individual who takes a round-the-houses approach. Neither strategy is intrinsically right or wrong, but they are different, and differences can cause discord.

Even small attempts to mirror another person's style can increase our sense of rapport. For example, when I'm talking to someone who is highly task oriented, I will start the conversation by explaining the intended outcome and then will provide options and recommendations. In this way, I am speaking their language, and it doesn't go unnoticed.

Understanding these characteristics is crucial for any teacher who wants to accelerate the learning of their students; it's also invaluable in customer service and sales environments. As you mirror someone's language, your sense of connection increases. When people are totally in tune during a conversation, they'll naturally start to mirror each other's body position, tone and language.

STEP 3:
Adapt Your Style
In the same way that you'd tune a radio to find the station you are looking for, consciously adapt your speaking and listening so that you are on the same frequency as other people.

Taking my own children as an example, one of them is highly reflective while the other two are extroverts. In contrast to the extroverts, it works best for my reflective daughter if I drop an idea into a conversation and then come back to it at a later point, allowing her time to consider things. This avoids arguments that would flare up if she felt she was being pushed into something without having time to mull on it. For my other two children, their method of processing tends to be the conversation itself. I'm better off asking them how they feel about a situation than what they think.

If the task of deciphering the preferred communication style of your friends, family and colleagues feels overwhelming, it's worth remembering that people are telling you their preferred communication style *all the time*, in *every* conversation. It all starts with paying attention to the way they speak and listen.

> *Lesson 13: Learn from people's language – it isn't random*

CHAPTER
FOURTEEN

ASK WHAT'S MISSING AND NEEDED

How to Avoid Getting into Blame

There's an ancient tale about two monks who were walking along a muddy road in the rain and found their way blocked by a small and fast-flowing stream. Unable to ford the torrent, a beautiful girl was standing at its edge, looking despairingly at the road beyond.

'Let me help you,' the older monk said without hesitation. Lifting the girl in his arms, he carried her over the stream.

The younger monk spent the rest of the day in silent contemplation, but when night came he couldn't contain himself any longer. 'What you did was wrong,' he said quietly. 'You know we aren't allowed contact with women. Why did you carry that girl across the stream?'

'I left the girl on the road,' the first monk said. 'Are you still carrying her?'[29]

The story offers a lesson about the way we might approach our conversations. We can either tackle them from a position of righteousness, which will lead to blamestorming, or we can look from the perspective of what's needed, with no judgement attached.

CRITICS AS DESIGNERS

For many years I worked with Mike Harris, an innovator who developed, launched and led three multibillion-pound brands. As a through-and-through entrepreneur, he's hardened to the fact that any revolutionary idea will be met with howls of derision from the watching world, along with all the reasons why it's doomed to failure.

'Why would anyone do banking over the phone?' cried the commentators in the late 1980s, when there was a bank on practically every street corner. Undeterred, Mike launched First Direct, the world's first major telephone bank. It's still winning awards, over 30 years later. Then he became chairman of a new mobile phone operator, declaring that 20 million people in the UK would eventually own a mobile phone. The critics laughed, but the business was later sold for $10 billion, and there are now 97 million mobile connections in use in the UK. Mike went on to announce the arrival of the world's first internet bank, leading the revolution in the online provision of financial services.

Understanding that people are inclined to offer negative judgements, Mike has learned to use this to his advantage by refining a theory he calls 'critics as designers'. Once he's developed an idea for a new proposition, he actively seeks out and listens to critics who'll tell him why it will never work. Armed with a list of their objections, he starts to investigate what's needed to address each of them successfully. For example:

Objection: Your telephone banking idea will never work because people hate being left on hold.
What's needed: Find a way to answer every call within three rings.

Objection: I can't stand it when I'm asked security questions on the phone, passed to a new adviser and then have to give my information again.

What's needed: When we pass on a caller, find a way to pass on their customer information, too.

Mike found that if people focus on thinking about what's needed, rather than wasting energy on trading opinions, it has a dramatic effect on their levels of motivation and productivity. When applied across an entire organization, this approach releases an explosion of energy and commitment.

In a similar vein, Steve Jobs, the CEO of Apple, was constantly asked how he managed to systematize innovation at Apple, presumably so that other people could copy his approach.[30] His reply focused on the way people conduct conversations. According to Jobs, the spark for brilliant ideas is more likely to come from impromptu corridor chats, late-night phone calls and ad hoc meetings than from formal processes or neat-and-tidy procedures. He knew that if he could paint a compelling picture of the future and challenge people to think about what was missing or needed to get there, he'd stand the greatest likelihood of success. While aspects of his communication style were highly imperfect, he was peerless when it came to understanding the secrets of innovation.

THE FOUNDATION OF LEADERSHIP

The world hushed for a moment on 11 February 1990 to hear Nelson Mandela speak.[31] He had just been released from prison after 27 years – 19 years of which were spent in solitary confinement. Would he use his freedom to set a tone of blamestorming and exact revenge on his oppressors, or offer his hand in reconciliation?

Just as Gandhi had done in August 1942 when he gave his 'Quit India' speech, Mandela held the future of a nation in his hands and resisted the temptation to opt for self-righteousness. He began by thanking the people across the world who had campaigned for his release and declared himself a humble servant who was placing 'the remaining years of my life in your hands'.

From then on, Mandela's speech was given over to explaining what he felt was needed. This included:

- The need to unite the people of South Africa in a single vision of the future.
- The need for the State of Emergency to be ended immediately and all political prisoners to be freed.
- The need for the future of the country to be determined by a body that was democratically elected on a non-racial basis.
- The need for 'our white compatriots' to join in the shaping of a new South Africa.
- The need for the international community to continue the campaign to stop the apartheid regime.

A 'what's needed' conversation like this is so powerful because there's no judgement involved. Mandela closed his speech by quoting the words he'd used on 20 April 1964 during his trial, where he'd stood in the dock facing the prospect of a life sentence or execution for sabotage, and expressed what he felt was needed:

I have fought against white domination and I have fought against black domination. I have cherished the ideal of a democratic and free society in which all persons live together in harmony and with equal opportunities. It is an ideal which I hope to live for and to achieve. But if needs be, it is an ideal for which I am prepared to die.

Another example of Mandela's legendary reluctance to engage in blamestorming occurred when he was called to the High Court to defend his decision to launch an inquiry into racism in South African rugby.

He was up against Louis Luyt, the president of the South African Rugby Union.[32] Their courtroom confrontation looked set to be a head-to-head collision. However, as soon as he entered the court Mandela walked over to Luyt's lawyers and shook their hands, while his representatives looked on in horror. Greeting your opponents wasn't exactly courtroom protocol.

Soon after, France's president, Jacques Chirac, arrived in South Africa and Mandela asked his assistant, Zelda La Grange, to invite Luyt's lawyers to a reception with the French head of state. It seemed an extraordinary gesture. Initially, she ignored his request until he became insistent that the invitation should be sent. Mandela had no interest in the tactics of self-righteousness. He was more concerned with what was needed to bring about unity in South Africa.

WHAT TO DO?

STEP 1:

Adopt 'What's Missing and Needed?' as a Thinking Practice

IT manager Ravi – who is husband to Mia and father to Yash, Ria and Jay – decides that for a complete day he's going to practise asking himself what's needed and scribble notes on it. This is what he wrote:

07.45

Yash comes into the kitchen in a foul mood, saying he'd get a better breakfast in prison. It's on the tip of my tongue to tell him to stop being an ungrateful brat. I think about what's needed and decide to talk to him tonight on the way back from football. I avoid a blow-up that would wreck the day and I mull on it on my way to work.

10.30

Steve [Ravi's manager] asks me whether I'm getting what I need from him. I'd prefer to avoid a difficult conversation and say everything's going fine, but when I ask myself what's needed, I decide to be honest. I say I'm concerned that he's operating at too low a level and I need more room to grow and develop. Tough conversation, but he says he's had the same feedback from someone else and promises to get better at letting go.

14.30

Chris [Ravi's colleague] tells me there's a problem with the delivery date on the new middleware release, and he complains that the sales team keep changing the parameters. Normally I'd jump straight in with advice, but instead ask him what he thinks is needed. It stops him in his tracks. After a bit of thought he says he needs to organize a meeting with all the parties to review the launch assumptions – a good way forward.

17.30

It's Mia's birthday the day after tomorrow, and I ring to check why her present hasn't arrived. I paid so it would arrive in three working days but nothing's been delivered. I'm given a lame excuse that it's been dispatched from the warehouse and is out of their hands. I almost shout, but I think about what's needed and ask to speak to a supervisor. When I get passed on, I explain in a level way that I feel misinformed and let down. The representative calls the delivery company while I'm on the phone and confirms they'll deliver tomorrow as long as someone's in to receive it. The supervisor says she'll refund the cost of the postage.

19.45

Bringing Yash back from football, I say he seemed grumpy this morning and ask him if he's OK. He says that yesterday he had a fall-out with a friend on the way back from school and that they sorted it out today. He says sorry for being a pain this morning. I think about what's needed in this situation and drop what I'd planned to say. He seems to have got the point and lecturing him won't help.

As you go through your day, keep asking what's needed. In doing so, you remove the drama and stress of blamestorming, allowing for more rewarding and constructive conversations. You'll also come up with different and more productive answers. If you can establish this as an ongoing practice in a work team, it will revolutionize the quality of your meetings, but it's no less potent in a family or community setting.

STEP 2:
Look from a Perspective of What's Important to You

When you ask what's missing and needed, it's vital to be clear what your reference point is. Bill is Daniel and Beth's next-door neighbour and he's well meaning but very quick to lean his elbow on the gatepost and offer the benefit of his advice. This can range from a broad-brushed commentary on the political landscape to a mini-lecture on how Daniel and Beth can improve their garden. Tact isn't his strength.

Here's an example where Bill catches Daniel:

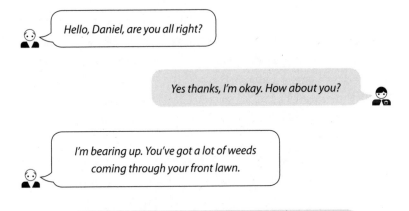

> *Hello, Daniel, are you all right?*

> *Yes thanks, I'm okay. How about you?*

> *I'm bearing up. You've got a lot of weeds coming through your front lawn.*

> *Oh, er … well, I suppose we've got a few. We haven't got around to tackling them yet – been a bit busy.*

You know how to get rid of them, don't you?

[sarcastically] How's that? Weed killer?

 Well, Daniel, you need to tackle them early, before they get deep roots and start to spread. It's important to get a spring feed for your lawn, which will kill the weeds and nourish the grass. I've got a friend who's a green keeper at the golf club and he's got a rule of thumb that he always sticks to…

Bill's sentences come in a continuous stream, without gaps between them; Dan grits his teeth. He doesn't like being called Daniel, and neither does he appreciate being given advice that he hasn't asked for. The situation is a difficult one, since Dan and Beth can choose their friends but not their neighbours. And when Dan complained to Bill that his cat was leaving its mess in the front garden, Bill appeared to take great offence and ignored them for a month.

We've all got a 'Bill' in our life, whether it's a neighbour, parent-in-law or work colleague. Some people spread their advice like confetti, regardless of whether we want it or not.

If you asked Dan for his opinions, he'd say that Bill is rude and obsessively interfering – and at times Dan would like to tell him so. However, if Dan looks from the perspective of what's important to him, it's to treat people with respect and to have good neighbourly relations. In light of this, he concludes that trust and relationship are missing and that what's needed is a different strategy for dealing with Bill.

When Dan remembers to look from the second perspective, he realizes that Bill:

- isn't badly intended or meaning to be insulting.
- can't see the importance of setting the context when he starts a conversation.
- doesn't realize that advice isn't welcome unless it's asked for.

When he remembers this, Dan doesn't take Bill's comments so personally. He decides that:

- He's not going to have a full-blown conversation with Bill about his manners – this doesn't seem necessary.
- He'll set the context if he needs to have any difficult conversations with Bill. By flagging where he's coming from, Bill is likely to be less prickly.
- He'll have a catch-up with Bill every so often to maintain good relations, but may need to cut the conversation short at other times. He can do this politely, saying that he's got a deadline, which is usually true.

Dan's decisions help remove negative feelings from the situation and give him a sense of control and responsibility; he no longer feels that he's the victim of Bill's behaviour. By returning to his values, and thinking about what's missing and needed for him to act in relation to them, he has a way forward that's more satisfying and has more integrity than avoiding Bill and complaining to Beth.

> **Lesson 14: Don't complain about what's wrong – ask what's needed**

CHAPTER
FIFTEEN

STRIVE FOR CLARITY

Why Checking for Understanding
Will Save You Time, Effort and Money

Many years ago, I loved seeing this notice in *The Observer*:

> *In the Review section's special summer reading issue of 2 July, we wrongly ascribed a reading list to Roddy Doyle, the celebrated Irish author. Unfortunately, owing to a misunderstanding, the 'Roddy Doyle' we spoke to, who gave us a very interesting selection of summer reading, was a computer engineer from north London.*[33]

This mistake didn't cause any harm, but the consequences can be far-reaching when the whole world is watching. The 2017 Oscars ceremony descended into chaos during its finale after Warren Beatty was handed the envelope for 'best actress in a leading role' instead of 'best picture', prompting the wrong winner to be announced.

For the 48 hours prior to the ceremony, only two people know the identity of the winners, both of whom work for the accounting firm PricewaterhouseCoopers. In 2017 it was the turn of Brian Cullinan and Martha Ruiz, who became minor celebrities in their own right. Cullinan described his role as 'the best job you can have as an accountant' and – when quizzed about the possibility of the wrong winner being announced – qualified his reply by saying, 'It's so unlikely.'

As the ceremony unfolded, Cullinan and Ruiz were stationed on either side of the stage. Each of them held a briefcase containing 24 envelopes, one for each Oscar category, allowing a presenter to be handed their envelope from either side of the stage. In a few fateful moments of inattention, Cullinan went from tweeting a backstage photo of Emma Stone to experiencing the full glare of the world's spotlight after getting his envelopes in a muddle. No lives were lost or animals harmed as a result, but the evening was described as a 'shambles of confusion, correction and contrition', and the reputation of the Oscars and the accounting firm were pummelled before the hysteria died down.[34] Organizations, communities and families are, in essence, a network of conversations; we coordinate our actions by communicating accurately. If we mishear someone, operate from false assumptions or provide the wrong information, the process breaks down.

REDUCE MARGINS FOR ERROR

There are times in life when we purposely obfuscate the message. If you want to make a romantic advance, playing a game of innuendo means you're less vulnerable to rejection, allowing you to evaluate the response and decide whether it's safe to make a more direct approach. Politicians create confusion by deploying the art of 'substitution' during interviews, by which they answer the questions they wish they'd been asked rather than the ones they were actually asked. This strategy is not confined to the political battlefield, since children use it to great effect with their parents and teachers, and it comes in handy at work, too. It's hardly surprising that we can be left scratching our heads or that the dynamics of conversation can feel frighteningly hard to fathom.

At other times an idea seems perfectly clear in our mind but comes out like a word salad when we try to express it. Mitt Romney was the subject of extensive press coverage for the following quote, attributed to him while he fought for the US presidency in the 2012 elections:

> *I believe in an America where millions of Americans believe in an America that's the America millions of Americans believe in. That's the America I love.*[35]

We may not sound as garbled as Romney but being able to communicate with clarity is a challenge for all of us. On top of this, it's never guaranteed that the people you are speaking to are listening anyway. How often have you been in a meeting in which someone's asked for a recap, only to hear back multiple versions of what was actually said? The solution for most everyday situations is to check your own understanding and ask people to confirm theirs.

For example, a recipe for confusion occurs while Diane's pulling together the information pack for the quarterly governors' board meeting at the primary school she heads up:

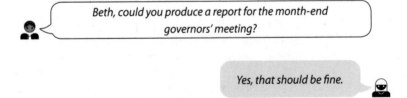

By changing the conversation slightly, Beth can reduce the likelihood of the Tangle ensuing. It might add 30 seconds to their exchange but would circumvent any potential areas of confusion and save the hours of lost time that might otherwise result:

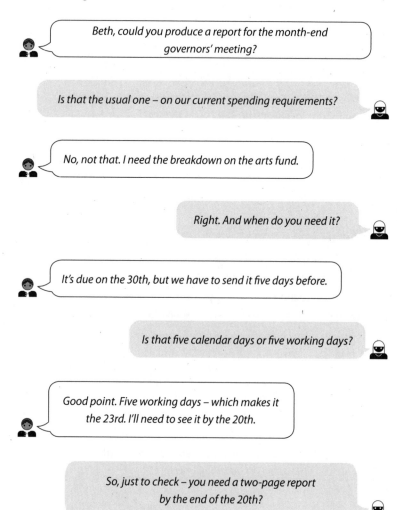

Beth, could you produce a report for the month-end governors' meeting?

Is that the usual one – on our current spending requirements?

No, not that. I need the breakdown on the arts fund.

Right. And when do you need it?

It's due on the 30th, but we have to send it five days before.

Is that five calendar days or five working days?

Good point. Five working days – which makes it the 23rd. I'll need to see it by the 20th.

So, just to check – you need a two-page report by the end of the 20th?

No, I only need 250 words. The two-page report is for the quarterly meetings.

> *Ah, right, now I'm clear. In that case,*
> *I'll do it by 5pm on Friday.*

Beth is pushing for clarity – just as well too, because she could have wasted time on a long report that wasn't necessary.

CLARIFY SPECIFIC ACTIONS

Beth's conversation with Diane raises a point about clarifying action. Some exchanges are only intended to provide information and context, with no specific follow-through expected. Others need to be formulated as a specific request if you want anything to happen. A note was sent out to the parents at my children's school asking them to generate support for an open day. It read like this:

> *We hope you don't mind us asking you for help, but wondered if it wasn't too much of an imposition if you might be kind enough to please forward this invitation on – possibly to friends, neighbours or work colleagues. It would be most appreciated, but of course you are under no obligation at all to do so. With many thanks in advance for your kind assistance and kindest regards ...*

It's not hard to decipher the subtext, which reveals an underlying concern about imposing. Unfortunately, it's unlikely to produce the desired effect. Without a clear request, you may as well sit on your hands and watch the world go by.

The same principle applies at work. I've sat in leadership meetings with companies that have tens of thousands of employees, and I have been aghast at the lack of rigour when it comes to conversations that need to produce action.

Ethan gets copied into the following email regarding an internal meeting at his bank:

Louis: Tuesday 12:44
Hi all. I would really like to get some time together
next week if possible. Which days would be good or if
next week is not doable what other dates do you have?

Matt: Tuesday 13:45
I've already got three hours blocked out on Monday
morning from 9am, which I thought was for a follow-up
to last week's meeting?

Louis: Wednesday 12:53
Sorry, the Monday meeting is changing from a meeting to
a Teams call and will not need attendance from you guys.
That said, it's still important that we get together.
Can we get a couple of hours next week?

Andrew: Thursday 07:53
Sorry folks. I'm struggling next week, and then I'm away
the following week.

In the end, the lack of a clear request for action meant that the meeting
never happened. Louis may have got a different result if he'd sent this email:

Andrew, Matt and Ethan,
To follow up from our meeting on Friday, we need two
hours together next week. By 6pm today, please would you
reply with your availability for Monday, Tuesday or
Thursday? In response, I will confirm the best day and
time by 10am tomorrow.

In this email Louis is being specific about what's required – two hours
next Monday, Tuesday or Thursday – and he asks for a reply by a given

time – 6pm today. He also gives a commitment to get back to his colleagues by a stated time tomorrow. By doing this, Louis has significantly increased the odds of a meeting happening.

Due to their sheer size, larger organizations are breeding grounds for confusion. Company strategies are based on hundreds of assumptions regarding the market, the spending power of customers, inflation, competitors and the anticipated success of future products. Many of these assumptions are hidden from sight for the majority of employees, meaning that the potential to get into the Tangle lurks in every conversation.

WHAT TO DO?

STEP 1:

Check for Understanding while Clarifying Your Own

Even if you think you've been clear in your communication with someone else, check that they've understood you. The same principle applies in reverse. Your understanding of what someone's said to you may not match what they actually said or meant. It could prove very useful, and there's no harm in saying:

Before you go any further, let me check if I've understood …

I ask this question at regular intervals during meetings and there are often diverse opinions about what's been said. Checking for understanding, as you go along, is good practice in any conversation.

STEP 2:

Check for Accountability and Action

However convivial, energizing or inspiring a meeting is, it won't drive things forward unless it involves clear conversations to generate and establish action. Three things need to be agreed to do this: exactly what will be delivered, by whom, and by when. If any one of these is omitted, the chances of the action being delivered as expected are drastically reduced. Practise this approach consistently and you'll see productivity increase. It's a small change that makes a considerable difference.

While some conversations can be loose and broad, others need to be sharp as a knife.

> *Lesson 15: It costs nothing to check for clarity, but it can cost a fortune not to*

CHAPTER
SIXTEEN

REMOVE INTERRUPTIONS

How to Focus on the Conversation You're Actually Having

There's a scene in the Disney film *The Jungle Book* where the boy, Mowgli, has been taken hostage by the monkeys and handed to King Louie, the orang-utan. It's up to Bagheera, a sensible and pragmatic black panther, to explain the rescue plan to Baloo, who's a rather irrepressible bear. Predictably enough, chaos ensues when Baloo gets distracted by the groove of the music. Dancing into the fray, all he can say is, 'I'm gone, I'm solid gone!'

Similar exchanges happen every day as we compete for the attention of people who are 'solid gone'. The battle to avoid interruptions and to focus on what's in front of us has become tougher in an age in which we're being bombarded by stimuli. Emails, texts, phone calls, instant messaging and advertising all seek to grab our attention. Managers come back from their holidays to find thousands of emails waiting for them. It gives them a dilemma: do they face a deluge of messages on their return or read them while they're away? Neither is a welcome option.

Interruptions can be physical intrusions that break our concentration or mental interruptions that disrupt our internal focus. Harvard University psychologists Matthew Killingsworth and Dan Gilbert used an iPhone application to gather data from 2,250 participants, aged 18 to 88, on subjects' thoughts, feelings and actions as they went about their daily lives. They concluded that people spend 46.9 per cent of their waking hours thinking about something other than what they're doing. What's more, their study drew a link between a wandering mind and an unhappy one.[36] The same principle applies to conversation: when we're fully present, both our conversations and our relationships are more stimulating and fulfilling.

The constant flow of information vying for our attention, much of it relatively subliminal, exposes us to more ambiguity than ever before – and this creates stress. Of course, the consequences of the information age are double-sided. The blurring of boundaries between work and home can offer remarkable opportunities in terms of flexibility and choice, but it also means that we tend to be less 'in the moment' in each environment. In turn, we begin to engage less in the tasks in front of us. We try to multitask, but there's evidence indicating that if a task requires any form of cognitive effort, multitasking means that it will take 50 per cent longer and include 50 per cent more mistakes.[37] We half-listen to others and are less attentive to the here and now. Over time we can end up feeling removed from the life we'd like to be leading.

SAWUBONA

There's a wonderful Zulu greeting that begins with someone saying 'Sawubona' – which means, 'We see you.' The response is 'Yabo sawubona' – which means, 'Yes, we see you, too.' It's an invitation to participate in

you carve it out. It's well documented that we're more effective and happier when we're fully absorbed in something. We'd all do well to re-learn this by watching young children focusing completely on what's in front of them, whether for a minute or an hour. It brings us back to Matthew Killingsworth and Dan Gilbert's assertion that a wandering mind is an unhappy mind.

By creating periods of uninterrupted time we become more engaged with life and with other people.

STEP 2:
Choose Your Time and Place

It's worth considering how your environment could become more conducive to good conversation.

As teenager Abby discovered when she chose the wrong moment to ask her mother to collect her from a friend's party, it's vital to consider the appropriate time and place for a conversation. Here are a couple of additional examples:

1. Beth wants to broach the subject of a pay review with Diane. She's nervous about mentioning it but Dan urges her to seize the opportunity at her next one-to-one, and they prepare together. On the day, Diane's previous meeting overruns. When she finally surfaces, she apologizes to Beth and says, 'Let's still have a quick catch-up, shall we?' Beth knows that the timing isn't ideal but has worked herself up for this moment and doesn't want to back out. As soon as she opens her mouth, she realizes it's a mistake. Diane is caught off-guard and says rather brusquely:

> *Oh ... I wasn't expecting that ... well ... I think we should talk about it at a later date. But I can't make any promises. Times are tough, you know.*

Beth realizes that she should have rescheduled the meeting. It's a classic case of right place but wrong time.

2. Lily, Ethan's mother, has something she wants to discuss with him. It's an important conversation for her, and she thinks she's found the opportunity when she goes with him and the grandchildren to the park. In her mind, she envisages the children playing so that she and Ethan are left to chat. As it turns out, her grandson Jack is charging wildly in all directions and granddaughter Anna is grumpy. Lily opens the conversation, but Ethan has to chase after Jack. She makes a second attempt, but this time Ethan has to deal with a disagreement over ice cream and Lily gives up the cause. The park turned out to be the wrong place. Afterwards, she's reluctant to bring up the subject again, in case it seems to Ethan as if she's pestering him, so she drops it altogether.

STEP 3:
Be Willing to Say No or Negotiate

When my son was at school, my wife Sally had an unexpected phone call from a tutor. The tutor said that he'd never previously experienced the difficulty he was having with Marcus. Sally feared the worst, but she was surprised by what followed.

'Here's the problem,' he explained. 'When I give Marcus his weekly homework, he negotiates!' Apparently, he would barter to do less English and more maths, or less of both. Afterwards, we talked to him about respecting authority and taking his work seriously, but privately agreed that his natural ability to negotiate – which was far more advanced than either of ours – would stand him in good stead and shouldn't be completely drummed out of him.

When he comes home from work, Ethan regularly says to his wife Lara that he's got nothing done that day. What he means is that he's been delivering on other people's priorities, which prevents him from progressing his own. Being able to say 'no' is as important a skill as any other in conversation. It's a requirement for staying in control of your life. If you say 'yes' to everything, you're at the beck and call of other people's demands. Just as it's easy to assume mistakenly that their own point of view is the truth, people are also inclined to think that their requirements are more pressing than anyone else's. Unless you're able to challenge, decline or negotiate the terms of an agreement before taking it on, you're likely to sink under the weight of accepted promises.

If someone interrupts you, make a conscious choice as to whether you'll put the activity you were engaged in on hold, or say you'll get back to them in five minutes – or half an hour, or later that day. Whatever your decision, the aim is to be fully in the conversation that you're in.

As we get to grips with our post-Covid world, in which flexible working has become the norm, I repeatedly hear people lamenting the lack of time and space for old-fashioned face-to-face conversation. The instinct for this is rooted deep in our psyche and for good reason.

Lesson 16: Being present is more valuable than being busy

REMEMBER TO EXPERIMENT

How Changing Your Conversations Can Revitalize Your Relationships

Defining the number of words in any language is a challenging exercise. Words go in and out of fashion and one word might have a variety of meanings. In addition, some words are considered to be obsolete while others are derivative. The *Oxford English Dictionary* contains full entries for more than 170,000 words that are deemed to be in current use. With the exception of people whose livelihood is tied to their vocabulary, most of us rely on a small fraction of the complete lexicon. We tend to build a limited and workable catalogue of words and then stick to it, without a great deal of curiosity or desire to extend it further. If you learned only 800 'word families' – root words and their various prefixes and suffixes – this would allow you to understand 75 per cent of the English language as it's spoken in daily life.[38]

The same principle applies when it comes to conversation – we tend to settle into a familiar pattern. Whether or not it works for us is a different matter. We may repeatedly have unproductive meetings at work with the same group of people, yet the familiarity of the situation somehow dilutes the urgency to do anything radically different.

Arguments also conform to well-worn pathways, accentuated by the fact that we develop biases that prime us to listen and respond to the world in preset ways. Changing these habitual behaviours isn't easy. Studies of patients who've experienced coronary bypass surgery show that the ratio of people who adopt healthier day-to-day habits after surgery is only 1 in 9 – even though the benefits of a changed lifestyle are crystal clear.[39] Why is this statistic so low? The answer is that we tend to opt for what we know, in preference to what will make a difference, and live for today rather than tomorrow. The same is true with conversation, in spite of the fact that consistently poor conversations will develop into unhappy relationships.

GETTING STUCK IN A RUT

At the weekend, Ethan and Dan meet and talk about their jobs:

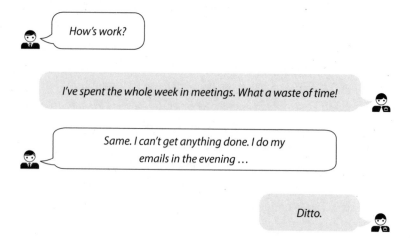

How's work?

I've spent the whole week in meetings. What a waste of time!

Same. I can't get anything done. I do my emails in the evening ...

Ditto.

… and then Lara goes mad.

I do my emails while Beth's marking homework. We've become the most anti-social couple.

I've fallen asleep twice this week reading a bedtime story to Anna – and she's gone downstairs and told Lara, 'Dad's snoring in my bed again.'

Although they have different family circumstances, Ethan and Dan are caught in patterns that don't seem to be working, but it's easier to stick with what's familiar than to make a change. When it comes to conversation, there are plenty of ways to do things differently. Here are some suggestions for shaking things up, all relatively straightforward to implement.

WHAT TO DO?

STEP 1:

Create New Rituals and Make Them Habits

Try folding your arms in the way you're used to. Now fold them the other way. It will feel wrong and, chances are, you'll revert to your old routine next time. In the same way, deviations in your conversational routines will feel awkward to start with, but persistent practice allows them to become seamlessly integrated into the sections of your brain where your habits are stored.

Here are some ideas to turn tired routines on their head. You could also try out some of your own ideas – the important thing is to find the ones that work for you and to persist with them.

At work:

- **For the first 30 minutes of your day, go and talk to people**: I recently read an article that said great leaders never start their day by wading through their emails. Whether or not this is true, it makes good sense. Emails tend to put you in reactive mode. In contrast, start your day in conversation. It creates relationship. Without this, nothing else will work.
- **Have 15-minute stand-up meetings**: These are the alternative to long meetings, where people settle in their chairs and happily give you their opinions about life. Stand-up meetings have a different energy to them; everyone wants to keep to the point. I've seen teams meet for five minutes every hour while under pressure on a project. It creates energy and focus and shows others that you mean business.
- **Don't fill the allocated time**: If you have a team meeting that's scheduled to be an hour in length, how come it always seems to last an hour? Why doesn't it finish early? It's because we tailor the conversation to fill the allotted time, rather than the other way around. Finish meetings early and give people some time back. They'll rarely complain.
- **Have lunch together and talk**: It's becoming increasingly common for people to grab a sandwich and eat lunch in front of their computer, or to email a colleague who's sitting a few desks away. Sometimes people laugh outright when I ask them how long they allow for lunch. We'd do well to learn from our continental cousins, who joke that 'you can always tell a Englishman by the crumbs on his desk.' They get together at lunchtimes to talk and have a complete break from their work. If you did this, the relationships you'd build would pay off over time.
- **Ask people what motivates them**: When was the last time someone asked you this question? It's perhaps the most important information for any manager, teacher or parent. Yet many people say they've never been asked it. Some people are highly motivated by achievement, success or money. For others, these have no bearing at all. They simply want to enjoy the journey and their relationships

with the people around them. Try asking – and then listen.

- **Reduce attendance lists**: Always start a meeting by asking, 'Does everyone really need to be here?' Don't wind up accumulating more and more meeting attendees. Life already contains enough committees without adding any more. And, if you don't know why you're in a meeting, don't stay – chances are that they'll cope perfectly well without you.

- **Get away as a team**: If it's within your power to make this happen, go away with your work team twice a year. Use it as a chance to catch up on each other's lives, review progress, talk about personal aspirations, create your long-term strategy and discuss how you're working together. It doesn't have to be a lavish affair – I've worked with teams in a remote hostel where we've slept in dormitories for a few pounds a night. It's the experience and the time together that count.

At home:

- **Ask for an alternative birthday present**: Take advantage of your birthday to ask for people to spend time with you. A friend of mine asks each of his grown-up children for one birthday present a year, and the same one every year – to spend a weekend with him at a location of their choice, where they can drink wine, talk and be together. Try this out and turn your phone off while you're doing it.

- **Do something away from home every week**: Conversation is easier when you aren't surrounded by all the jobs that need doing. Getting away is hard when you have young children, but you can offer to look after your friends' or families' children for an evening, or even a weekend, in exchange for them doing the same for you. When you do get away, you may need to agree a ban on spending all your time talking about the kids – or the household chores.

- **Eat where you can speak**: It's a fact that fewer than a third of US families eat dinner together regularly.[40] Of those who do, more than half watch a screen at the same time, which acts as an effective conversation killer. This is an area that requires clear family ground rules. Maybe TV dinners can be the exception rather than the rule.

- **Put your phone away completely while you talk**: This principle applies equally at home and at work. Psychologists at the University of Essex conducted experiments on the impact of having a mobile phone in view while conducting a conversation.[41] Feelings of closeness and trust were reduced when a mobile phone was placed between the participants. You can test this principle for yourself by looking at your phone several times while someone's speaking to you, and then asking them what it feels like. If they're honest, they're likely to say they felt ignored or undervalued and struggled to hold your attention. Putting your phone away – completely – is the remedy.

- **Acknowledge each other more often**: Our taste buds are much more sensitized to bitter tastes than sweet ones, since bitter tastes are more likely to be toxic and need immediate rejection from the body. In the same way, negative feedback and criticism are more 'sticky' in our minds than praise or acknowledgement. As a consequence, we're liable to complain that someone 'never has a good word to say about us' or that our partner 'always finds something to criticize'. We can balance the scales by consciously finding ways to acknowledge them. This doesn't require you to pour out vacuous praise, but means being on the lookout to offer encouragement and thanks whenever they are due. While doing their ground-breaking research in the Love Lab in the 1970s, John Gottman and Bob Levenson found that for every negative interaction during a conflict, a stable relationship has five or more positive interactions. This can include expressing affection, offering appreciation and demonstrating that their partner matters.[42]

- **Consider conversation as an aphrodisiac**: I once attended a corporate dinner during which a colleague turned to me after a couple of drinks and said, 'The greatest aphrodisiac for my wife is to go out for a coffee, shoot the breeze, and for me to listen to her.' This comment came directly after a discussion about the leadership requirements of his business, and was a bit of a surprise, but he's by no means unique. Women have been telling their partners the same for decades, yet somehow it fails to compute in a male brain in which listening is not the obvious antecedent to sex. However, men will also testify to the fact that there are few things in life that create a greater sense of connection – and experience of love – than being heard.

There's no need to shake up every part of your life, but it's worth examining any areas where your conversations have gone stale. Remember, occupying the same space as someone else is not the same as actually talking together. The challenge is that people have different needs. Those of us who are more reflective need time on our own to recharge our batteries. I met one mother who said that after a full day of interacting with clients and colleagues at work, she needed an hour on her own every day. It wasn't that she didn't love her family, but she didn't have the energy to engage with them until she'd had some private time. For her husband, the opposite was true. He got his energy from engaging with her, so they had to work out a method for both to get their needs met. This is where conversation comes into play again, enabling us to understand each other's perspective and resolve differences in expectations.

While it's true to say that changing your thinking can in turn revolutionize your behaviour, it can also work the other way round. Developing new behaviours can lead to different ways of thinking. This happens in a literal sense – new neural pathways in the brain are opened up, heralding the potential for new opportunities.

STEP 2:
Learn from Your Mistakes
A friend who teaches the violin took on a young and highly gifted student. During their first lesson she asked the student to play a piece of her own

choice. Except for a brief moment when she stumbled on a note, the girl played exquisitely. My friend was impressed that she'd been able to recover her poise and continue with no further mistakes. The student, however, was appalled at her error and burst into tears. The incident demonstrated why the girl was struggling to progress – she thought she had to be note-perfect, believing that was the sole hallmark of a great musician. It was probably the consequence of previously being told that she had to 'get it right' and being scolded whenever she didn't.

Striving for mastery in any field has to involve learning from mistakes, and conversation is no exception. If we're honest, we conduct very few conversations that we could claim are close to perfect. More often than not, we're left reflecting on how we could have spoken up more assertively or listened more attentively. The marvellous thing about conversation is that it's fundamentally messy and essentially creative, and continually changes direction. The sooner we embrace this understanding, the more we can surrender to it, enjoying the process of experimenting and learning on our way to excellence.

If we can learn from what doesn't work, we can become ever more expert, without expecting to reach an ultimate destination. While 'doing the same thing over and over and expecting a different result' is a popular definition of insanity, trying new approaches to conversation really is the secret to improvement – as long as we learn from our mistakes.

Lesson 17: Don't fear mistakes – learn from them

CHAPTER EIGHTEEN

TALK ABOUT
MENTAL HEALTH

Make it Safe to Say 'I'm Not Okay'

People sometimes ask me why I have specialized in the dynamics of communication. In response, I tell them my own story.

I grew up in a stable family, with parents who were deeply loving and caring. Without exception, everyone who knew my mother referred to her as a saint, and my father was the most honourable man you could wish to meet. I did nothing to earn such good fortune and have been immeasurably lucky.

At the same time, my parents were the product of their time, growing up in the shadow of two world wars. I remember quizzing my grandfather, Donald, about his experiences during the First World War, asking tactless questions as only a child can. He was always quick to change the subject, choosing not to recount how he'd been shot on the opening day of the Battle of the Somme in 1916, along with 60,000 other British casualties. As for my paternal grandfather, Maurice, he never talked about the pain of losing three quarters of his men to death or imprisonment – while also fighting a heroic rearguard action and retreating to the beaches of Dunkirk. Like so many of his contemporaries, he stuffed grief and pain into the dark recesses of his being, in the hope that it would dull and eventually fade. It didn't.

Against this backdrop, it's hardly surprising that my parents' generation were reluctant to talk about their feelings. My father became a senior-ranking officer in the military and had to deal with loss and heartbreak as part of his job. I remember the phone ringing one Sunday lunchtime, and hearing news that our next-door neighbour had been killed by a roadside bomb. Dad took a deep breath and went next door to tell the man's widow – a mother of four children, including newborn twins – while we stared at our plates of food and Mum held her head in her hands. Many years later I asked Dad how he had dealt with mental health challenges amongst his men and their families. 'It didn't come up,' he replied.

THE COST OF SILENCE

Just as my grandparents and parents struggled to express their feelings, so did I. Being in a military family meant that we had an itinerant life, packing our belongings into wooden crates every year or two, as 'home' changed from Europe to Africa to Asia. As a consequence, I went to boarding school at the age of eight, as my brother and sister had done before me.

I vividly recall being dropped at the front door on my first day at school. My dad shook my hand – hugging didn't feature in his upbringing – and said he'd see me in a few months. I quickly concluded that I needed to hide feelings of homesickness from public view. Even when I went home for the holidays, I would tell my parents everything was fine at school and change the subject, especially if I was struggling.

It was only during my university years that I started to appreciate the cost of withholding my state of mind. Dad rang me one evening to inform me that my grandmother had died and, when pressed on the matter, admitted that it was ruled a suicide. It turned out that she had made previous attempts to end her life, but we hadn't been told, even though we were adults. My grandmother didn't want to bring shame on the family, and I felt so distressed that she had carried the stigma of depression in silence.

Following my grandmother's death, I resolved to catch up on lost time and start communicating with my family. Since love was assumed rather than expressed in my family, I wrote a card to my parents thanking them for everything they had done for me and saying that I loved them. As I heard the card drop into the post box, I was overcome with fear that my words would be met with silence.

I was right. Over the following week or so, I would regularly check my answerphone and post, but heard nothing. Eventually, I rang my parents but avoided mention of the card, and we had a chit-chat as if nothing had happened. 'Here we go again,' I told myself as I put the phone down. It was only a while later, when I went to see them in Norfolk, that something unexpected occured. My mother took me into the kitchen, out of earshot from my father. 'You'll never guess what happened on Valentine's Day,' she whispered. 'For the first time in 40 years, Dad sent me a card saying that he loved me!'

Funnily enough, the card I'd sent was never mentioned – even though I could see it on the mantelpiece – but that wasn't the point. A seed had been sown and, over the following year or two, we experienced a genuine transformation in our family relationships. Taking encouragement from those early gains, I gave my father a hug the next time I saw him, and he eventually became the best hugger in the family. In his twilight years, he communicated his love for us whenever we spoke.

I recount this story as a reminder that small expressions of love, appreciation and concern can cause profound and positive ripples in the lives of the people around us.

WHAT TO DO?

STEP 1:
Invest in the Relationship

Every conversation has a relational dimension. Even if the topic is trivial or transactional, we still need to manage the tone and manner in which we conduct the interaction, and be responsible for the impact we may be having on them.

I once sat on a train and heard a man talking to his ex-partner on the phone about their son, who appeared to be at boarding school. He evidently felt that the teenager wasn't putting enough effort into his studies, and I braced myself when he said, 'Right, I'll give Joe a call.'

The man's opening line to his son went like this:

Joe, it's your father. Have you got your exam results?

It's easy to criticize other people's communication style, but I couldn't have scripted a worse start. He was overly formal, obviously irritated, and made no effort to get into his son's world. His subsequent questions were:

What was your mark for history?

Did you answer all the exam questions?

Did you do enough revision for it?

Are you going to come and see me sometime?

The man seemed displeased with his son's answers, not least the reply to his final question, and their call ended quite abruptly. I knew nothing about the history of their relationship, but I could predict the teenager wouldn't be visiting his father anytime soon.

It saddens me that a conversation like this can be so damaging for people's sense of connection, and yet small changes could have made a meaningful difference. Imagine if Joe's father had asked questions like this:

> Joe, it's Dad here. How are you? [LISTENS]

> How are you feeling about your exam results? [LISTENS]

> Right...so you feel disappointed about your history result? Where do you think it went wrong?

> I'd love to see you sometime during the holidays.

My point is that every conversation is an opportunity to invest in the relationship, and it starts with taking an interest and bothering to listen. Over time, this creates a reservoir of trust and affinity.

STEP 2:
Ask How People Are *Really* Feeling

According to the World Health Organization, approximately 280 million people in the world suffer from depression.[43] The resulting feelings of emptiness, hopelessness and even thoughts about dying or suicide are bound to influence the way people communicate. For example, someone suffering from depression may become more withdrawn and use language that indicates they are struggling to cope. In short, there are warning signs, if only we can pay attention to them.

Like my grandmother, many of us feel ashamed to say that we are struggling and have well-grooved mechanisms for hiding our true feelings. When people ask how we are, we have a stock lexicon of about six words for replying to the question, 'How are you?' In response, we say something along the lines of 'Okay', 'Alright', 'Good', 'Great', 'Fine', or 'Not bad', which is usually code for 'Terrible'.

We resist expressing ourselves because we don't want to burden people, especially when their question is intended as a courtesy rather than a genuine inquiry. However, given the modern-day challenges we face in relation to stress and mental health, perhaps we need to develop strategies for going deeper.

As a single mother and a headmistress who is attuned to managing staff and pupils, Diane is conscious that she needs to keep investing in her relationship with her teenagers, Abby and Ben. She makes a concerted effort to ask them about their day, and to listen non-judgementally when they share about the ups and downs of their friendships. Even though her mind tells her that she has much more important things to do, Diane makes this conversation her absolute priority, even just for a few minutes. She knows that 'Okay', 'Good' and 'Great' are not always a true reflection of how Abby and Ben feel, and has developed a wide array of questions such as:

You've looked a bit down this week. How are you feeling?
Did something happen at school today?
How did that make you feel?
You said that you're dreading next term. Can you tell me more?

Based on Gallup's Global Emotions Report (2022), 330 million adults go at least a fortnight without talking to a single friend or family member.[44] Finding out how someone feels can making a life-saving difference when it comes to their mental health. When my son Marcus worked in a supermarket during the Covid-19 epidemic, we impressed on him the importance of connecting with each customer, however briefly. As they came to his till, he would say hello and ask, 'How are you?', before pausing for a second or two. Some of them hadn't spoken to another soul for weeks, and even a simple gesture allowed people to feel seen and heard.

If someone seems particularly stressed or makes a comment that leaves me concerned about their mental health, I try to engineer a conversation to find out more. If I come across them in the workplace and don't know them well, I'll speak to their manager or a colleague who's close to them. If they're a friend, I may speak to them directly or to one of their family members. Without claiming to be a mental health expert, I can signpost people to professional support. The worst option is not to say anything.

STEP 3:
Share Your Own Story

Being vulnerable is never easy. To let our guard down, we must let go of the idea that we need to be strong, coping and happy. Not long ago, my daughter spent hours consoling a friend who was distressed about the state of her life, only to see an Instagram post that evening by the same friend declaring that her life is amazing. Somewhere along the line, we bought the idea that we must put on a good front.

Yet the statistics prove that many of us are struggling to thrive in a world that's become more complicated and mentally demanding than ever before. Our brain and nervous system are taking the brunt of this impact, which in turn can affect our emotional state and our mental health.

We can make it easier for people to speak up by sharing our own story. I spend many weeks each year with construction workers who – historically at least – have operated in a macho environment, in which sharing your feelings was viewed as a sign of weakness. Over the last year or two, I've talked more openly about the challenges in my own family than ever before, from the demands of caring for my father after he fell down the stairs and suffered brain damage, to the deterioration in my sister's mental health that led to her tragic and untimely death. I have been deeply touched by people's responses. Rather than being met with a wall of silence, I've witnessed more honesty, compassion and authenticity than I could have imagined. Life brings its fair share of ups and downs, and it would be a tragedy if we had to hide our vulnerability. It all starts with a willingness to say, 'I'm not feeling okay.'

> **Lesson 18: Share your humanity – it could save a life**

CHAPTER
NINETEEN

CROSS THE THRESHOLD

How to Find Your Voice and Speak Up

In his brilliant book *On Chesil Beach*, Ian McEwan tells the story of Edward and Florence falling into blame and recrimination on their wedding night. In the opening scenes they make excited small talk about the future, but there's a dark subtext in the form of unvoiced concerns about sexual difficulties and the inability to listen to each other.

Despite her love for Edward, the prospect of a physical relationship inspires a sense of dread in Florence, but she's unable to express her fears. Edward's desire for Florence is almost overpowering, but his unspoken dread is that he'll let himself down by producing a below-par performance on their first night. Sure enough, their encounter in bed turns into a disaster; Edward 'arrives too early', prompting Florence to flee in panic to the beach. When Edward catches up with her, their survival instincts take over.

Edward accuses Florence of having no idea how to be with a man, the worst form of discounting. Florence follows suit, and her response goes against the grain of her character and her true feelings for Edward when she makes a mocking comment about his sexual failure. Aware of the damage she's done, Florence makes a last-ditch effort to repair the situation. She suggests Edward should fulfil his sexual desires with someone else. Edward can't see this for what it is – a desperate attempt to secure his love – and is outraged. When he finally arrives back at their hotel room, Florence is gone. Wedding presents are returned by post and a divorce is confirmed on the grounds of non-consummation. In an hour or two, they have got themselves into the Tangle, the Big Argument and the Bad Place. Faced with this predicament, and ill-equipped to deal with it, Florence has opted for the Lockdown.

THE COST OF WHAT WE DON'T SAY

The tragedy of Edward and Florence's story is that they don't voice their underlying fears and concerns. Much of the time it's what we don't say that causes the problems.

Returning to the cargo ship *El Faro*, which sank in October 2015 with the loss of all hands, the voyage data recorder (VDR) tells the heart-wrenching story – sentence by tragic sentence – of a crew who felt powerless to challenge their captain. The officers on the bridge talked at length about the prospect of the vessel sinking, but only when the captain was out of earshot. When speaking to him directly, they softened their words.

With the benefit of hindsight, the second mate, who was also the ship's navigator, needed to say something like this:

Captain, I'm concerned for the safety of the ship and crew if we hold our course. My recommendation is to change course via the Old Bahama Channel or take an alternative route.

Instead, the second mate said this:

> Do you want me to just steer the most … the course that's the most comfortable ride … or just stay on course – stay on track?

There were multiple opportunities for members of the bridge team to challenge the captain directly, but they all backed off. As weather conditions became more extreme, the chief mate asked:

> So what did you say? … There could be a chance that we could turn around?

Failing to decipher that his subordinate was making a plea rather asking an innocent question, the captain replied:

> Oh, no no no. We're not gonna turn around – we're not gonna turn around.[45]

In both instances, the crew members asked a question instead of making a direct request and pulled back from expressing their true anxiety. From the safety of my keyboard, it's easy to blame them for not speaking more directly, but I can count numerous times when I've done something similar, albeit in situations where there weren't so many lives at stake. Courage is the choice to cross a psychological threshold and find our voice, without knowing what the outcome will be.

A FRIENDSHIP ON THE LINE

Let's take Mia and Lara's relationship as an example. They're old friends, and in their early 20s were practically inseparable. But circumstances have changed and they're both married with children now. Ravi and Ethan have little in common, so they don't tend to meet up as families. Lara has tried to contact Mia a couple of times recently about getting together on their own, but Mia's been unable to make it. She also cancelled a get-together at short notice. Lara's last text said:

```
Hi M. Hope all's well. Haven't seen you for AGES!!! Can
we catch up soon?? L xxxx
```

Mia would love to see Lara but at the moment she's struggling with life's demands. While Lara has time to meet during the day, Mia is over-stretched at work. Her team is under-resourced and they're dealing with an incredibly stressful legal case. Meanwhile, evenings and weekends are taken up with the children's homework, football, judo, dance classes and more. When she finally replies to Lara, she says:

```
Oops sorry. Things mad here. B in touch soon.
M x
```

Lara's negative bias kicks in and her thought process goes like this:

> *But this is what you said last time, and you didn't call then. Your text doesn't seem like the kind of message you'd send to one of your oldest friends. It's more like something you'd send to an acquaintance. You used to be so amazingly reliable about keeping in touch; now I'm lucky to get an 'x' at the end of your text – if you reply at all. Maybe you've moved on from our friendship. Maybe Ravi doesn't want us to get together because he doesn't get on with Ethan … Maybe he's got a chip on his shoulder because Ethan's more successful than he is. It shouldn't always be down to me to contact you.*

Over the days that follow, Lara's 'maybes' become fixed views. Everything seems to be pointing her to the conclusion that Mia has moved on and isn't interested in their relationship any more. Lara even goes through her diary and discovers she's only met up with Mia once over the past nine months. During that time she's sent Mia seven texts but only had four back and one of those was to cancel their get-together.

Conclusions work in a very particular way: they take the grey out a situation so that we know how to respond. In doing so, they determine the world we see. Said another way, we see the world through the lens of our conclusions and collect evidence to support them.

In the end, Mia does get in touch and they do organize a get-together. However, Lara's unsure whether or not to raise the issue. Here are two scenarios that could unfold for her:

Scenario 1: The thought of talking about how she feels seems awkward to Lara, so she holds back. They have a perfectly nice catch-up, but it's as though the basis of their relationship has somehow changed. Of course they're still friends, but it doesn't feel as though they're special friends – and this is what hurts. Lara's not sure what she's done wrong and she decides to back off from initiating contact with Mia.

Scenario 2: Lara decides to raise the issue with Mia and thinks about how to tackle the conversation. She makes real efforts to set up the context and to express her feelings rather than her opinions. She also endeavours to be responsible for her own story and begins as follows:

> *Listen, I really hope you don't mind me raising this, but I miss not seeing you more often. We used to be in touch all the time. I know we've both got families and absurdly busy lives, so it's not going to be like the old times when we were single. I've been wondering whether you've moved on from our friendship or if there's a problem. Or have I just made all that up?*

Mia is very surprised to hear this, but the conversation doesn't escalate because Lara's done a superb job of opening it and ensuring there's no sense of accusation. What happens next is an outpouring from Mia, particularly about the stresses of work, none of which Lara was aware of. It turns out that the legal case has been a horrible ordeal. A client has been suing social services for negligence, involving members of Mia's team directly; she had to testify at the tribunal. As if that wasn't enough, they've found out that Jay has dyslexia and dyspraxia. It's not a huge problem, but it explains his disaffection with school and issues with his coordination. Their conversation enables Lara to take the second perspective on what's been happening, and completely alters her view of the past few months.

Before they leave, Mia apologizes for not including Lara in what's been going on in her life. Lara realizes that her earlier conclusions were a complete misunderstanding. She'd got into the Bad Place, but it now feels as if her issues have been completely resolved.

Crossing the threshold isn't easy, particularly when it's a difficult conversation about sex or infuriating personal habits or deep-set fears. It's important to remember that 'difficult' is a relative term. What's easy for you may be challenging for me and vice versa. Some subjects may seem too trivial to broach and you'd feel ridiculous doing so. Others can feel too hard. You may worry that raising the problem will cause deep offence and an irreparable faultline in the relationship.

On the other hand, if you don't speak up, the problem may become so magnified in your mind that it starts to have an impact on your relationship. This can lead to your not speaking – or meeting – as often as you used to, or feeling a sense of distance when you do, or losing contact completely.

There's really no comfortable middle ground; there are consequences to speaking up and consequences to keeping quiet, and life doesn't come with a warranty that another person will be willing to talk. However, when we do cross the threshold and speak up, as Lara did, it's often less traumatic than we'd feared. When my children were young, I experienced a gnawing concern that I was letting them down in my role as a father, because my work involved so much time away from home. I resolved to talk to them, yet noticed I was fearful of the outcome; it was ridiculous, perhaps, but I didn't want to discover that my concerns were founded. In the end, I chose my opportunity to speak to Emily, our eldest. Our conversation went like this:

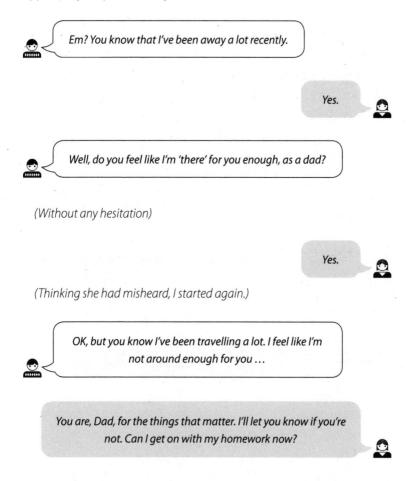

> Em? You know that I've been away a lot recently.

> Yes.

> Well, do you feel like I'm 'there' for you enough, as a dad?

(Without any hesitation)

> Yes.

(Thinking she had misheard, I started again.)

> OK, but you know I've been travelling a lot. I feel like I'm not around enough for you …

> You are, Dad, for the things that matter. I'll let you know if you're not. Can I get on with my homework now?

My other children, Rosy and Marcus, echoed Emily's sentiments. It was evident that I'd made up a story in my mind about how I was failing in my role. Of course, the solution was to cross the threshold and ask them. This principle is at the heart of *Watch Your Language* – you can assume that you know what someone else is thinking or feeling, but you don't for sure until you've asked them. Said another way, don't always believe what you think.

WHAT TO DO?

STEP 1:
Separate Impact and Intent

Lara could have avoided getting into the Bad Place if she'd been able to distinguish between impact and intent. Here's how it works.

When something has a negative impact on us, we're inclined to think that the other person is badly motivated or has ill intentions. The more we feel hurt, let down or angry, the more we tend to blame the other person or question her motives.

In Lara's mind, it works like this:

> *I feel hurt and let down. Mia doesn't value our friendship.*

Lara's far less likely to think like this:

> *Mia has no wish or desire to cause me any hurt and
> yet I feel hurt and let down.*

This statement may feel like a contradiction in terms, but it's much more accurate than the first one. Separating intent and impact helps avoid getting into mental tangles.

In Edward and Florence's case it might have saved their relationship. Years on from their fateful night on the beach, and after a subsequent marriage and divorce, Edward recognizes what actually happened with Florence. He realizes that her intentions were selfless, even rather extraordinary. The impact of her proposal had been tremendous, but this didn't mean that she'd been duplicitous. If he'd been able to recognize this in the moment, he might have been reassuring rather than self-righteously indignant.

By the time he understands what happened, Florence is long gone.

STEP 2:
Make a Choice

There isn't a law that demands that you speak up when you have an issue or problem in a relationship. Perhaps over time an immediate issue may become less significant. But, either way, it's important to make a choice in the here and now.

You can either choose not to address the difficulty and be responsible for the consequences, or choose to cross the threshold and speak up. If you decide to go with the latter, pay careful attention to giving the conversation the greatest chance for success, rather than going down the path of trying to prove that your assumptions are right.

STEP 3:
Speak up

If you decide to speak up, there's nothing worse than beating around the bush. I don't mean that you should skip the context and go straight for the jugular. Some people pride themselves on being straight talkers who will tell you what they think whether or not you want to hear it, considering it your problem if you don't like what you're told. This works well for some people, while others will be offended, particularly when there are different cultural conventions at play. A straight-talker's intentions may be sound, but the impact can be negative.

It's important to adapt how you speak depending on who you're talking to and according to the situation. As Lara found with Mia, there are times where we need to drop the pretence and make the conversation real. Sometimes it's the conversations we don't have that sink our relationships.

STEP 4:

Give People Space

By the time you get round to having that difficult conversation, you may have given considerable thought to what you want to say. In contrast, it may come as a complete surprise for the recipient. Be prepared for the fact that they'll need to come to terms with what they're hearing.

In her 1969 book, *On Death and Dying*, Elizabeth Kübler-Ross introduced a hypothesis based on her work with terminally ill patients. In the majority of cases she found that patients went through a spectrum of different emotional states: beginning with denial then leading to anger, bargaining, depression and acceptance. Her model has since been adapted to fit a broader set of situations in which someone receives unwelcome news. The instinctive response is often to deny it, followed by feelings of anger, then withdrawal to lick their wounds and, finally, coming round to acceptance – whatever form this takes and whatever the timeframe.

Whenever you give difficult feedback or cross the threshold to address an issue, you need to give people room to voice their thoughts and feelings. If you listen to them, they're likely to reach the acceptance stage more swiftly.

Lesson 19: There's a risk to speaking up and a cost to staying silent

CHAPTER
TWENTY

UNDERSTAND YOUR IMPACT

Why Words Move Life – for Better or Worse

Our lives are constantly being influenced by conversations – and we're not even involved in most of them. Right now, politicians and other policymakers are having interactions that will have far-reaching implications for our career or the amount of taxes we pay. Take Liz Truss for example, who became prime minister of the United Kingdom in September 2022, announcing sweeping tax cuts at a time when concerns about the national debt were already rampant. Her words wiped 80 billion pounds off London's blue-chip FTSE stock index, prompting her to offer her resignation after 44 days in office and become the shortest-serving prime minister in British history.

Prior to Liz Truss, the archetype of self-destruction in British folklore was Gerald Ratner, who nearly bankrupted his company when a joke backfired. Having spent 25 years building his family jewellery business into a household name, he wiped £500 million off its share value during a speech to 5,000 people at the Institute of Directors. In his speech, he referred to a cut-glass sherry decanter with six glasses on a silver-plated tray that Ratners were selling for £4.95. 'People ask, "How can you sell this for such a low price?" I say, "Because it's total crap."' Adding insult to injury, Ratner commented that the earrings his shops sold were 'cheaper than a Marks & Spencer prawn sandwich but probably wouldn't last as long.' Just a few words cost Ratner his £650,000 salary and slashed his billion-pound turnover in seconds. His speech features in Stephen Weir's book, *History's Worst Decisions* – along with Eve eating the apple and Nero destroying Rome.[46]

On a personal level, conversations can help us make decisions, inspire us, deepen relationships and encourage us to get things done. When they go wrong, though, we can end up feeling hurt, misunderstood or betrayed.

CHICAGO TO LONDON

Some while ago, I was travelling on a night flight from Chicago to London. After a long week away in a different time zone it was a relief to get airborne. We were on schedule and I was aiming to get the 7am train home from the airport for a late breakfast with the family on Saturday morning.

We were more than halfway there when my neighbour alerted my attention to the screen on the back of the seat in front of him. On the display he was pointing at, the map of our plane's progress seemed to show that we were flying directly away from our destination – to Newfoundland, Canada. Other passengers had realized this too and a wave of discontent was sweeping through the plane. People stood up, intercepted flight attendants and started impromptu conversations in the aisles. Reactions ranged from annoyance to alarm and fury.

Suddenly, above all our chatter, the captain's voice broke through on the intercom. I don't know if voice-tests are part of the selection procedure for pilots, but this one had the textbook tone of a flight captain. Immediately, we were all ears.

Some of you will have noticed that we have changed direction. I'm sorry to say that a passenger at the front of the plane is ill and requires immediate medical assistance. We are flying to St John's in Newfoundland, where medical staff will be waiting. It will take us about two hours to get there and then we'll need to refuel before setting off again. I apologize for the disruption this will cause to your journey but thank you for your patience. I'll update you in due course.

The pilot's announcement only lasted for about 30 seconds. It confirmed long delays yet, in that moment, a transformation took place in the way passengers were behaving. Despite the news of the detour, the atmosphere in the cabin suddenly changed. The general mood became one of acceptance, support and concern for a fellow passenger whose life was at stake. As we approached St John's we were diverted slightly northward to Gander, where we eventually made our landing. Even though the sick person was further up the plane, and we couldn't see anything, we sat in silence as we heard the thump of the doors opening and the sound of the paramedics rushing on board to attend to her.

When we took off again, resuming our journey to London, there were no complaints. Nor, when the plane had landed, did people start rushing for the exits. I felt a quiet pride in our dignified response and a respect for the pilot. He'd made the decision to take 200 people on a two-hour return rather than continuing to London for three or four hours. Although not long, those two hours could have given our fellow passenger the extra time that made the difference between her living or dying. It was the right call to make and we all knew it.

On the train home from the airport, I reflected on what had happened. The captain's announcement had been both brief and factual. I wondered why it had precipitated such an instantaneous change in our attitude and behaviour, and I realized that it was the meaning we'd created from his words. The captain's message formed a bond between us and in our minds we became partners in a flight to save a life. Any personal discontent dwindled into insignificance.

MEANING-MAKERS

The fact is that we humans are meaning-makers and languages of all kinds – visual and verbal – are our primary tools in the construction and reinforcement of meaning. This can work to our advantage or against us. When it comes to conversation, our storytelling brain creates significance out of what people say and what they don't say, from the way they phrase their words to the way we read their body language. A slightly raised eyebrow, a comment that tails off, a subtle change in tone or a choice of word can lead us to conclusions that may or may not be in line with the other person's intentions. It's what makes conversation so challenging, dynamic and endlessly intriguing.

In his classic book *Organizing Genius*, Warren Bennis outlined the characteristics of what he called 'Great Groups' – groups of people who've collaborated in a way that allowed them to achieve remarkable accomplishments, defying historical precedents in the process. Bennis argued that the leaders of these groups create 'missions from God.' This doesn't mean that they find religion; rather, they create an extraordinary sense of collective purpose. Instead of operating within existing industries, they invent new ones. Rather than being constrained by rules, they redefine them. You won't find them saying that they spend their day 'having meetings'; they're working out how to change the world. In short, they use conversation to imbue their endeavours with meaning.

On the other hand, an unwise word, or the absence of a word, can work against us. President George W. Bush must have regretted a response that he gave on a golf course after receiving news of a suicide bombing: 'I call upon all nations to do everything they can to stop these terrorist killers.

Thank you. Now watch this drive.'[47] With these words he continued his round of golf, leaving a media storm behind him.

Bush's comments may have been totally sincere, and yet his pause between 'terrorist killers' and 'Now watch this drive'– separated with a 'thank you'– was too brief. The listening world concluded that for George W. Bush, golf took precedence. The difference between compassion and dispassion can be measured in the length of a single breath.

The greatest leaders understand the profound impact conversation can have and seek to master its skills. The best sports coaches are no different, learning when to acknowledge someone's efforts and when to challenge them. Wonderful teachers take the same approach. Test this by casting your mind back to your school days. Which teachers killed your interest in a subject? They might have been technically proficient, but it's likely that they were pretty dry and monotonous. They may not have lacked the power of speech, but they probably lacked proficiency in the art of conversation and any skill in speaking and listening. We've all had teachers like this, but also one or two who held our interest and sparked our curiosity.

With these inspiring people, we were motivated to learn and develop – we probably owe them a debt of gratitude for our subsequent life decisions and relative success.

WHAT TO DO?

STEP 1:
Discover How You're Doing

Find out what impact your conversations are having on other people. There have been instances in my work when I've asked a manager how an important conversation with one of their staff has gone. 'Yeah, it was great,' came the reply. But the report from the team member didn't concur at all. They felt lectured and spoken down to – ending up in the Bad Place.

The best way of finding out how effective your conversations are is by asking. It's a relatively simple thing to do but we often avoid asking in case we find out something we don't want to hear.

Benjamin Zander is a founder and conductor of the Boston Philharmonic Orchestra. He gives the members of his orchestra a white sheet of paper in every rehearsal so they can offer comments, ideas or feedback. Start adopting the same principle. Following a work conversation you have with a peer, perhaps during the next day, ask if they have any thoughts or insights they didn't mention the day before. Then listen. If they take the opportunity you've offered and give you feedback, you'll invariably learn something useful. And if you take action based on what they say, they're more likely to offer unprompted feedback next time. It's a way of developing relationships based on a sense of trust and partnership.

STEP 2:

Start with Yourself

David Marquet, author of *Leadership is Language*, tells a compelling story of turning followers into leaders while commanding a nuclear submarine. He was appointed to lead the *Sante Fe*, a submarine that had the worst attrition rate and safety record in the US fleet. Twelve months later, the *Sante Fe* recorded the best results ever seen and their officer retention rate increased from 0 per cent to 100 per cent. How come?

In short, Marquet created an environment in which people felt that their voice counted. He encouraged divergent thinking and challenges to the status quo, and he gave people complete authority to make decisions that were appropriate to their role. Marquet calls this a leader-leader approach as opposed to a leader-follower approach. As he changed the way he conversed with the crew, they began to communicate differently with him and with each other, which in turn changed the culture and transformed their results. There isn't a paint-by-numbers formula because human environments are far too chaotic for that, but the point is this: Marquet started with himself. Like Amy Sutherland, who stopped blaming her husband Scott for his shortcomings and applied strategies used by exotic animal trainers, we all have a sphere of influence. As Marquet says, 'What is leadership but language?'

If we start with ourselves, and acknowledge our impact on the people around us, the ripple effect stretches into the very fabric of our lives and our relationships.

Lesson 20: Conversation moves life – that's why we invented it

TAKE ON A LIFETIME OF PRACTICE

Why Practice Is More Important Than Perfection

There's a cartoon which shows Tarzan preparing to traverse the treetops to announce his love to Jane. He practices an eloquent speech and then swings over to her on a leafy rope. When he opens his mouth, all that comes out is, 'Me Tarzan, you Jane'. All of us have experienced our own version of this. We start a conversation with a clear intention, and then fail to follow our plan.

The English conductor Sir Thomas Beecham used to tell a story of forgetting someone's name. He was walking down the street one day when he met a woman he recognized. Unfortunately, he couldn't for the life of him remember who she was, so he pretended to know her while asking questions that, he hoped, would reveal her identity. After discussing the weather and other pleasantries, he enquired after her family and was told that her brother had been poorly. Taking this as his cue, he asked what her brother was up to. 'He's still King,' replied Princess Victoria.[48]

We all have times when, for one reason or another, we muck up a conversation. We get people confused with each other, make unfortunate comments, email the wrong person or fall victim to the aberrations of predictive text. I once wrote a message to a senior executive in which I referred to 'the thing' I'd sent him; he was a bit surprised to see me asking if he'd received 'the thong'.

LEARNING FROM OUR MISTAKES

Of course, some conversations count more than others, and therefore the cost is higher when we get them wrong. Many people say that they fear public speaking more than death, which sounds quite extreme, but proves that it can invoke genuine terror.

I had my own near-death experience in this regard, and it gave me sleepless nights for weeks. I was asked to give the keynote speech at a large conference, and was genuinely excited at the opportunity, but felt out-of-kilter in the run-up to the conference. The night before, while staying at the venue, I slept poorly and began to feel unwell. I considered pulling out altogether, but people were already arriving, and I decided to tough it out.

The next morning, after a glowing introduction which made me sound like Superman, I stepped up on stage and spiralled into a state of genuine panic, to the point that I wasn't sure if I could stand up any longer. If a genie had offered me a wish in that moment, I would have opted for spontaneous combustion. An hour later, when the last question had been asked, I nearly ran off the stage.

That afternoon I was chairing a board meeting, and I arrived in a state of distress. When I told my colleague what had happened, he said, 'Oh man! You look broken.' Later that day, Sally used the exact same phrase.

As it turned out, my client was very gracious about my performance. It was far from a raging success, but it wasn't an unmitigated disaster either – I had managed to turn it into a catastrophe in my mind. Over time, I realized how attached I had become to my professional reputation. It was my image of myself – my identity – that had been broken, and I experienced a kind of liberation on the other side of it. Perhaps I could stop being so driven towards success, allow more room for mistakes and even bear the occasional failure.

The author Richard Rohr, who started life as a Franciscan friar and has become one of the great spiritual thinkers of our time, refers to this as shadowboxing. Rohr recommends that we practise shadowboxing on a daily basis, which requires us to face our contradictions, catch glimpses of our vanity and embrace our humanity. In recent times I have learned to talk about my vulnerabilities more than my strengths, and the authenticity and depth of the ensuing conversations has been humbling and rewarding.

CONTINUAL IMPROVISATION

When you consider the complexities involved in having a conversation, it's surprising that we don't make more mistakes. Since we don't have direct access to other people's thoughts, we have to rely on the difficult art of language – and meaning construction – to convey our pictures of the world to each other. This process is both remarkable and highly imprecise. People don't say exactly what they mean, so we're constantly trying to fill in the gaps in our understanding in order to create a coherent picture from the pieces we're given.

To help the process, we evaluate a multitude of non-verbal cues while trying to hear what they're actually saying and simultaneously pulling together our own thoughts in preparation for a response. Once we become the speaker, we use our personal lexicon to convey our views and opinions before another switch occurs. It all happens at lightning speed – like a downhill skier adapting, in each moment, to the conditions under his feet. For most of the time we take this process for granted, and it's a testament to the miracle of the human brain that it usually works so seamlessly. However, it consumes vast reserves of energy – which explains why you can spend a day in meetings and feel physically wrecked at the end of it.

People admire actors who can improvise on the spot, often saying they couldn't possibly do it themselves. In reality, we're all in the business of improvising. Conversation demands it because we don't know for sure how other people will react and we have questions that can't be answered in advance. If I speak my true feelings, will I get rejected? If I challenge my manager, will my career be cut short? If I raise that issue with my friend, will she take offence? We make internal predictions about the likely outcome and our negative bias is inclined to convince us it's safer to avoid speaking up. The long-term costs include love not getting expressed, issues not being addressed and damaging conclusions being drawn that create fault lines in our friendships.

There are no guarantees that a conversation will turn out for the better if you speak up. However, it is possible to increase the odds that the outcome will be successful.

DESTROY THE MYTHS

To start developing your skills in conversation you'll need to dismantle some popular myths:

Myth 1: you're either good at conversation or you're not. Some people are naturally more social and extroverted than others. They may speak confidently but, bearing in mind that conversation requires both speaking and listening, this doesn't mean they're better at it. Whatever your character, you can always improve. And, unlike the double bass player or pianist, who would struggle if they wanted to take their instruments everywhere with them, conversation can be practised wherever there's a person to speak to.

Myth 2: conversational skills can't be taught. It's true that conversational skills tend to be developed through trial and error, in the hustle and bustle of daily life. But it's also true that you can take them to another level if you're willing to develop new techniques and engage in mindful practice. Let's take our memory as an analogy. Many people say that theirs is like a sieve, yet the world's greatest memory champions claim that their innate memory is no better than anyone else's. They simply practise tried-and-tested techniques that allow them to tap into the brain's unused potential for filing and recalling information. 'Anybody can do it,' says Ben Pridmore, a former world champion who once memorized 27 packs of cards in an hour. Similarly, when it comes to conversation, the same benefits are available to all of us, if we can be bothered to invest our time and effort in ongoing practice.

Myth 3: talk is cheap. Saying that talk is cheap is no different to saying that wine is cheap; it can be, but it can also be wildly expensive. Some conversations will have little impact on the direction of our lives while others will have a lasting effect – for better or worse. We've all experienced the benefit of conversations that have gone right, as well as the cost of conversations that have gone wrong, from friendships to relationships or job interviews.

Myth 4: I'm too old to change. The idea that you're too old to improve is nonsense. As long as we're able to speak and listen, we have the capacity to improve. In a passport control queue at a Spanish airport, I once overheard people in front of me laughing with the official – a rare occurrence. As I stepped forward, I saw two officials, side by side, in the smallest of security cabins. In age, they were probably approaching 60. One of them looked at our passports and then, in broken English, explained what they were doing: 'We try to better make our English,' he said. 'Can we practise?' Rather taken aback by this unfamiliar routine, I nodded and waited to see what would happen next. Drawing his shoulders up, he announced in his best possible accent: 'The formula for shopping is that way! And the formula for the plane is that way!' This little exchange made my day and reminded me that it's never too late to learn.

WHAT HAPPENS NEXT?

Once you've debunked the myths, it's all about practice. Over time, this is what happens:

- Daniel and Beth learn to develop their skills. Like high divers who can prevent injury by pulling out midway through a routine that's gone wrong, they find that it's possible to press the stop button during arguments that are becoming toxic. With the benefit of a little space and reflection, they adopt the second and third perspective and drop the domineering. They're more conscious about the impact of comparisons and threats and use them with their eyes open.
- Diane finds that she gets a better reaction from Abby and Ben when she expresses her feelings rather than her opinions. Sometimes she forgets and flies off the handle, prompting the Big Argument, but these occasions are becoming fewer. She finds that if they create clear agreements, the process of resolving an argument becomes easier and that she and Abby are less often on tenterhooks with each other.
- Ethan and Dan realize that Lily is quite lonely and often just wants to be listened to. When they listen to their mother instead of trying to fix her problems, they don't get into the Tangle. On the other hand, when Dan is speaking to Bill, who's addicted to fixing, he understands that Bill's intentions are harmless, even though his words can be insensitive.
- When Lara and Mia manage to resolve their differences, their friendship becomes stronger than ever. In fact, it feels unbreakable because they

are confident that they'll be able to engage in difficult conversations whenever they need to.

There is no Hollywood fix for any of these characters. Life doesn't work like that, and conversation is too messy to provide a perfect ending. On occasions they're all still prone to shotgun responses, which lead to the Bad Place, the Tangle and even the Lockdown.

However, when this happens, they're equipped to repair the situation through their subsequent conversations. Increasingly, they find that they can have mindful interactions in which they notice and respond to the warning lights as they appear.

Speaking for myself, I've had numerous times since this book was first published when I've forgotten how to listen. When this happens, my wife Sally will say to me, 'There's a good book you should read, by a guy called Rob Kendall. You'd find it useful.' I've mostly learned to take this as feedback.

WHAT TO DO?

STEP 1:
Stay Humble
I've already referred to my meeting with Tim Gallwey a number of years ago. To me, he represented the epitome of an effective coach. During a group session with him he asked us what score, out of 10, we'd give ourselves as a coach of others. I considered the depth of my experience and weighed up whether I should give myself an 8 or an 8.5. As we went around the room, most people offered scores in this region – after all, we considered ourselves to be quite accomplished in our field. Someone had the presence of mind to ask Tim how he'd score himself. He gave himself a rating of 6.5. At this point we suddenly felt as though we'd massively overshot in terms of our own self-evaluation.

That day was a lesson for me and it's been borne out in my experience;

the more I learn, the more I still have to learn. Rather than being an endless source of disappointment and frustration, this realization is hugely liberating. I can stop trying to be perfect or a know-it-all or indispensable. I hope that I can contribute, to the best of my abilities, while still stretching to improve further. As George Bernard Shaw said, 'The single biggest problem in communication is the illusion that it has taken place.' If I keep this in mind, it helps me to stay humble.

STEP 2:
Keep Practising

As a student, I wrote a dissertation on Henri Matisse. He became one of the finest artists of the 20th century, despite displaying little ability or interest in art during his youth. In fact, while he was studying for his law exams in Paris, he didn't even visit the Louvre. It wasn't until he was recovering from appendicitis at the age of 21, when he was given a box of paints to help him convalesce, that he ended up painting, and continued to do so every day for the next 60 years.

While Matisse would admit that aptitude has a role to play in being a great artist, his story is a victory for application over born genius. In the months before his death in his mid-80s, he was still stressing the importance of both maintaining a curious mind and being dedicated to practice.

Reading his letters and interviews, it is clear that his sense of freedom became more intense as he became more curious. He made no apology for being a lifelong student at heart. Despite the fact that his work hung in galleries all over the world, he found the idea that he'd mastered his medium laughable.

The same could be said in relation to conversation. After another 30 years of practice, I hope to become really good at it.

> **Lesson 21: Conversation is a process, not a destination**

NOTES

Chapter 1

1 The *Oxford English Dictionary* says that conversation involves talk, and it defines the verb 'talk' as 'speak in order to give information or express ideas or feelings; converse or communicate by spoken words'. I am creating a wider definition of conversation, to reflect the fact that we are increasingly communicating in new ways. In doing so, I am moving closer to the original Latin word *conversari* which meant to 'keep company'. The current meaning of the verb 'to converse' only emerged in the early 17th century

Chapter 2

2 The shotgun response is referred to by Daniel Kahneman as the 'mental shotgun' in his outstanding book, *Thinking Fast and Slow*, Farrar, Straus and Giroux, New York, 2011. He is describing the brain's continual assessment of threat levels and our generation of immediate answers in which speed of response and energy conservation take precedence over accuracy or mindful thinking

Chapter 3

3 'Samuel Goldwyn, Biography', IMDb, www. imdb.com/name/nm0326418/bio

Chapter 4

4 Taken from 'How to Get Along for 500 Days Alone Together', BBC Online News Magazine, 1 March 2013, www.bbc.co.uk/news/magazine-21619765

Chapter 5

5 Stephen R. Covey read this quote by Viktor Frankl in a library book at a university in Hawaii, but didn't make a note of the source. A full account is available at www.viktorfrankl.org

6 The Air Florida Flight 90 report can be found in the National Transportation Safety Board 'Aircraft Accident Report', 13 January 1982. See www.ntsb.gov/investigations/accidentreports/reports/aar8208.pdf

7 For the full story of this tragedy, read Rachel Slade's excellent book, *Into the Raging Sea*, 4th Estate, London, 2018

8 Ten Colossus machines were in use by the end of the Second World War, decoding encrypted messages between German High Command and German army commands across Europe. See bletchleypark.org.uk/our-story/75-years-since-colossus-arrived-at-bletchley/

Chapter 6

9 From Dr Alan Porter's letter to *The Times*, reprinted in *The Week*, 7 January 2012

10 For Huey Long's filibusters, see www.senate.gov/artandhistory/history/minute/Huey_Long_Filibusters.htm

11 Elizabeth Stokoe dedicates a full chapter to the 'conversational racetrack' in her book *Talk*, Robinson, London, 2018

12 See the full report (2021), based on surveys with 2,180 young adults, at www.princes-trust.org.uk/about-the-trust/research-policies-reports/youth-index-2021

Chapter 7

13 Numerous articles document the case of SM including: www.nationalgeographic.com/science/article/meet-the-woman-without-fear
14 The basis of Damasio's book, *Decartes' Error*, is that science has overlooked emotions as the source of a person's true being. He argues that emotions are essential to rational thinking and social behaviour

Chapter 8

15 Gallwey's book turned the prevailing thinking on sports coaching on its head. See *The Inner Game of Tennis*, Jonathan Cape, London, 1975

Chapter 9

16 This illusion is named after its discoverer Hermann Ebbinghaus (1850–1909) and was popularized in a textbook by Edward B. Titchener in 1901
17 Amy Sutherland, 'I Trained My Husband Like an Exotic Animal', *The Week*, 7 October 2006. The article first appeared in *The New York Times*

Chapter 10

18 For a full transcript of Geoffrey Howe's speech, see www.ukpol.co.uk/geoffrey-howe-1990-resignation-letter-to-margaret-thatcher/
19 For a definition of unparliamentary language in the UK parliament, see www.parliament.uk/site-information/glossary/unparliamentary-language/
20 From the indexes of the New Zealand Parliamentary Debates, www.parliament.nz/en/visit-and-learn/history-and-buildings/special-topics/unparliamentary-language/
21 A summary of their findings can be found at www.gottman.com/about/research/couples/

22 Official statistics for casualties during the construction work for the Olympic Games state the following: 1996 Barcelona = 2 deaths; 2000 Sydney = 1; 2004 Greece = 14; 2008 Beijing = 10; 2012 London = 0. See 'London Olympics Construction is Safest in Recent Times', *Engineering News Record*, 30 July 2012, www.enr.com/articles/2643-london-olympics-construction-is-safest-in-recent-times
23 See 'To Have and to Hold ... for 87 Years!', Mail Online, 1 November 2012, www.dailymail.co.uk/femail/article-2226145/Worlds-longest-married- couple-Husband-wife-100-spent-87-happy-years-together.html

Chapter 11

24 The 2020 Gallup Q12 Meta-Analysis Report can be downloaded here: www.gallup.com/workplace/321725/gallup-q12-meta-analysis-report.aspx

Chapter 12

25 According to a survey of 1,100 people conducted by Esure, quoted in Brendan O'Neill, 'Sorry to Say', BBC Online News Magazine, 8 January 2007, news.bbc.co.uk/1/hi/magazine/6241411.stm
26 From Plato, *Apology* trans. Benjamin Jowett
27 Shakespeare, *Macbeth* Act 2, Scene 2

Chapter 13

28 *Mama's Last Hug*, Granta Books, London, 2019, p. 92

Chapter 14

29 Story told by Zen Buddhist monk and scholar Hara Tanzan (1819–92).
30 From an interview with Jobs in *Business Week* in 2004, reprinted in 'Steve Jobs: In his own Words', *Telegraph*, 6 October 2011, www.telegraph.co.uk/technology/

steve-jobs/8811892/Steve-Jobs-in-his-own-words.html

31 For the full text of Mandela's Cape Town speech see: archive.nelsonmandela.org/index.php/za-com-mr-s-16

32 See John Carlin, 'Mandela's Rock (Part Two)', *Guardian*, 8 June 2008, www.theguardian.com/lifeandstyle/2008/jun/08/women.nelsonmandela

Chapter 15

33 The story is recounted as 'Roddy Doyle Ha Ha Ha?' and can be found at anecdotage.com/anecdotes/search?q=Roddy%20Doyle

34 The full story of the fateful Oscars mix-up can be found at eu.usatoday.com/story/life/2018/02/28/we-were-there-how-worst-flub-oscar-history-went-down/377305002/

35 As the Republican party's nominee for President of the USA, Romney had a habit for quirky quotes. See www.washingtonpost.com/blogs/compost/post/mitt-romney-self-deports/2012/01/23/gIQAHNtnNQ_blog.html

Chapter 16

36 See Steve Bradt, 'Wandering Mind Not a Happy Mind', *Harvard Gazette*, 11 November 2010, news.harvard.edu/gazette/story/2010/11/wandering-mind-not-a-happy-mind/

37 See R.D. Rogers and S. Monsell, 'Depth of Processing and the Retention of Words in Episodic Memory', *Journal of Experimental Psychology: General*, 124(2), 1995, pp. 207–31, Table 2 of Experiment Cluster #1

Chapter 17

38 See www.bbc.co.uk/news/world-44569277

39 David Rock and Jeffrey Schwartz, 'The Neuroscience of Leadership', Strategy + Business, 43, 2006. See

davidrock.net/wp-content/uploads/2016/06/Rock__Schwartz_sb_43_06207.pdf

40 See Harvard Graduate School of Education article here: www.gse.harvard.edu/news/20/04/harvard-edcast-benefit-family-mealtime

41 A.K. Przybylski and N. Weinstein, 'Can you Connect with Me Now? How the Presence of Mobile Communication Technology Influences Face-to-Face Conversation Quality', *Journal of Social and Personal Relationships*, 30(3), 2013, pp. 237–46, first published online 19 July 2012

42 For more detail see www.gottman.com/blog/the-magic-relationship-ratio-according-science/

Chapter 18

43 For up to date statistics on depression see www.who.int/news-room/fact-sheets/detail/depression

44 For the Gallup Global Emotions Report (2022) see www.gallup.com/analytics/349280/gallup-global-emotions-report.aspx

Chapter 19

45 For the full El Faro investigation report see www.documentcloud.org/documents/3237729-El-Faro-VDR-Audio-Transcript-8510451-ver1-0-page-130

Chapter 20

46 Stephen Weir, *History's Worst Decisions*, New Holland, London, 2009

47 This comment was made famous by Michael Moore's 2004 documentary, Fahrenheit 9/11

Chapter 21

48 This possibly apocryphal story is recounted at en.wikipedia.org/wiki/Thomas_Beecham

FURTHER READING

Bennis, W. and Biederman, P.W., *Organizing Genius*, Nicholas Brealey, 1997

Bohm, D., *On Dialogue*, Routledge, 1996

Carlin, J., *Playing the Enemy*, Penguin, 2008

Flam, J., *Matisse on Art*, Phaidon, 1973

Gallwey, W.T., *The Inner Game of Tennis*, Jonathan Cape, 1975

Gottman, J. and Silver, N., *The Seven Principles for Making Marriage Work*, Weidenfeld & Nicolson, 1999

Harris, M., *Find your Lightbulb*, Capstone Publishing, 2008

Kahneman, D., *Thinking Fast and Slow*, Farrar, Straus and Giroux, 2011

Lee, N. and Lee, S., *The Marriage Book*, Alpha International, 2000

Mandela, N., *The Long Walk to Freedom*, Little, Brown, 1994

Stokoe, E., *Talk*, Robinson, 2018

ACKNOWLEDGEMENTS

It is nearly a decade since the original version of this book came into print. Robert Kirby at United Agents believed in me when others didn't, and Owen Smith allowed me to find my literary voice. The team at Watkins have provided tireless support since 2014, and I owe special thanks to Fiona Robertson and Brittany Willis.

For this edition, I am most grateful to Andy Powrie and Rosy Kendall who generously gave their time and editorial input.

Writing books occupies countless hours that could otherwise be family time. It is only the most generous of souls who can retain a sense of humour while urging me to continue on such an uncertain journey. My wife Sally and our children, Emily, Rosy and Marcus, have given me the room to express my voice and follow my path. It is my aspiration to do the same for them.

ABOUT THE AUTHOR

Rob grew up in a post-war era in which families struggled to express feelings, difficult conversations were routinely avoided and the term 'mental health' was whispered behind closed doors. Coping with acute shyness and spurred on by experiencing the impact of suicide in his family, Rob sought to understand the art and skills of effective communication and to share his learning as widely as possible. He's worked on every continent and with people from all walks of life, from the powerful and privileged to those struggling to put a meal on the table.

Watch Your Language was previously published as *Blamestorming* (2014), an award-winning book which has been translated into multiple languages. It was followed by *Workstorming* (2016), a survival guide for having effective interactions in the workplace.

Rob has delivered consulting work for more than 75 organisations, and appears frequently on radio and in national newspapers.

He has been married to Sally for 32 years and has three grown-up children.

For more information, visit www.conversationexpert.com